Getting Your Children Sober

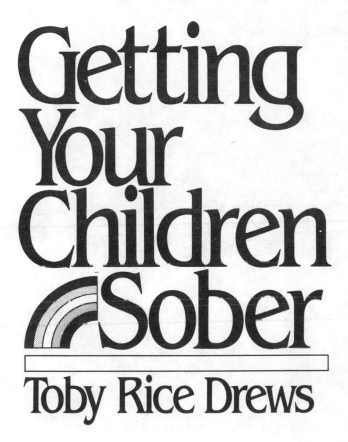

Getting Your Children Sober

Toby Rice Drews

BRIDGE PUBLISHING, INC. • SOUTH PLAINFIELD, NEW JERSEY

Also by Toby Rice Drews available from Bridge Publishing, Inc.:

Getting Rid of Anxiety and Stress
Getting Them Sober, Volume 1
Getting Them Sober, Volume 2
Getting Them Sober, Volume 3

GETTING YOUR CHILDREN SOBER

Copyright © 1987 by Toby Rice Drews
Library of Congress Catalog Card Number: 87-71392
Bridge Publishing, Inc., 2500 Hamilton Boulevard
South Plainfield, New Jersey 07080, USA

ISBN 0-88270-637-3

Printed in the United States of America
First Printing: October 1987

TABLE OF CONTENTS

ACKNOWLEDGMENTS

I want to offer very special thanks to these people whose special sharing helped me write this book:

William Hawthorne, M.D., Executive Director of Spofford Hall, Medical Director of the Mediplex Group and member of the faculty of the Harvard Medical School.

James R. Milam, Ph.D., author of *Under the Influence*, and co-founder of the Milam Recovery Centers in Bothell, Washington.

Trish Morphew, Senior Program Consultant for Adolescent Treatment, CompCare Corporation.

Pat Myers, a consultant for adult children of alcoholics and Executive Staff Member of the Renaissance Treatment Center in Minneapolis, Minnesota.

Jeri Schweigler, Ed.D. of the National Training Associates (League of IMPACT Schools) in Ukiah, California.

Gerald D. Shulman, Ph.D., Vice President of Clinical Programming of the Addiction Recovery Corporation of Waltham, Massachusetts.

Dolly Stephenson, C.A.C., Community Relations Representative of the Recovery Centers of America and a member of the Governor of Maryland's Advisory Council on Alcoholism.

And all the wonderful recovering alcoholics and families who generously gave me their time and their stories in hope of being part of the awakening process of our fellow survivors.

FOREWORD

by Carolyn Burns,
Vice President
National Federation of
Parents for Drug-Free Youth (NFP)

Toby Rice Drews has given parents gentle, practical and do-able answers in *Getting Your Children Sober.* This book is *must* reading by any parent who suspects their child might be using alcohol or other drugs.

As Toby points out, parents don't need to feel guilty, but they need to get appropriate help for both themselves and their children. The problems of drug and alcohol use among our youth has now reached epidemic proportions with millions of youngsters experimenting with drugs before the age of twelve. In a recent *Weekly Reader* survey, 25 percent of fourth grade students said they feel "some" to "a lot" of peer pressure to try beer, wine, liquor, or marijuana. By the time they are in seventh grade, about 60 percent feel pressure to try alcohol, and about 60 percent, to try marijuana.

While working with the National Federation of Parents for Drug-Free Youth I have answered calls from thousands of parents who were concerned about their children's use of drugs: children who abused their parents both physically and verbally, children who didn't come home at night, children who were having problems in school, children who had attempted suicide. These were parents in pain, watching once bright, energetic, happy children become lethargic, uninterested in family relationships, and no longer living up to their potential.

These parents were scared. They may have recently found beer bottles and drug paraphernalia and were panicked and disbelieving, or they had hung in there with their children for years with things only seeming to get worse. Their marriages were in trouble, their stomachs hurt, they were depressed.

I am convinced parents don't have to stay stuck in these situations. There is hope and help available for both the parents and their children. In this wonderful book, Toby shows how parents can be released from the guilt they are bound to feel when a child becomes an alcoholic or addict.

The most important thing a parent can do is to face reality, find a support group, and save themselves from the craziness that is bound to occur when there is a family member who is chemically dependent. When one person in a family relationship changes, the whole relationship changes.

I believe that for most parents, the addiction of a child can be more painful than the addiction of a spouse. Detachment from the disease of alcoholism and addiction comes much harder. Often there is the sense of having failed as parents.

The good news is that there is hope. By persevering, by learning about the disease and its effect on families, by putting the principles of this book into practice—you *can* move from despair to finding answers and serenity.

INTRODUCTION
Why This Book Is Needed

This book is for all parents who are frightened by their children's behavior. Equally, it is for all parents who are frightened by their own feelings toward their children. It is also for those parents who are frightened by a lot of advice they may already have received from professionals—be they school counselors, therapists, or alcoholism and drug experts—admonishing them to "get control of their children now." Such "helping professionals" often seem not only impatient with parents, but even *angry* at them for their inability to immediately get their children into treatment.

In *Getting Your Children Sober*, I will show you that you absolutely have not caused your children's drinking or drug problem; that addiction is hereditary; that no matter what you do, or have already done, you cannot "make a person into" an alcoholic or drug addict. You may have tried all the "proper parenting" methods available, presenting very good "role models" for your children, and that would not have caused or prevented your child from developing an addiction. And I will show you, with gentleness, how to find practical relief and real help for you and your children.

This book, too, is for all professionals who counsel parents and their children. For too long, helping professionals have demanded of parents too much too soon by neglecting their confusion, their guilt, and their terrors.

I have lived with the disease of alcoholism all my life. For a number of years, I maintained two separate yet concurrent careers, in writing and in college teaching. When in the 1970s, I developed and taught curricula for several universities on "Alcoholism and the Family" these three elements—writing, teaching, and alcoholism—somehow came together.

I understood that the non-alcoholic spouse of the alcoholic was an invisible, hurting, terrorized person with tremendous, unmet needs. And I understood much more about alcoholism. The enormous worldwide response to my first book, *Getting Them Sober*, validated that understanding, and I feel privileged that I have been part of the solution.

For the past few years, though, I've noticed that no matter how wonderful self-help and professional counseling groups are, parents find that they cannot "let go" of their *children's* problem as easily as they could their *spouse's* (or brother's or sister's). They cannot so easily reduce their fear of their children's dying, or worries about losing their children's love—the bond is much stronger.

Many parents I've spoken with around the country have learned about and tried "tough love". Basically, this concept means not protecting one's child from any of the consequences of his or her actions, with the hope that these consequences will be so painful that the child will accept treatment and change their behavior. Tough love, when used synonymously with intervention, also can mean confronting the alcoholic—usually as a group comprised of significant family members and friends and an alcoholism counselor—making the alcoholic go to treatment.

But most parents can't "get tough" with their kids. Parents want to *love* their children, not, as they see it, *reject* them. So it makes sense that the vast majority of parents cannot carry out a concept such as tough love, as it has been presented to them.

Over and over again, parents tell me, "I can't do that to my child. She'll run away from home and die in the streets!" or "He'll be so angry with me. I can't bear the anger that's there *already*, so how can I bring on any more!"

6

I do not believe that it is of any use to try to force terrified parents to do what I, as a counselor, want them to do, before they are ready. Why? Because parents then leave therapy, at a point when they are often so despairing, that they are never heard from again. Counselors tell me, "But the kid could get hurt or even die if I don't force the parents to *do* something!"

I believe that most parents are so scared that making them feel guilty pushes them into doing nothing.

In this book I will explain how counselors can use an extra few weeks or months in counseling to *gently* help parents to be *able* to intervene with their children. And I will show parents how to ensure that they get the kind of help—and time for help—they need.

I will present methods I have successfully used with my clients that *do* work in getting the vast majority of parents to begin to see, face, and deal with their children's alcoholism—methods that help them shed guilt and fear, and realize some control over their own lives and the lives of their children.

Most parents want not only information but concrete suggestions. "What do I do *now*, right this minute?" they ask. To meet this need, I have included at the end of each chapter a few very simple tasks for parents. The tasks are divided into two categories:

"Write on" questions help parents recognize and understand how they actually have been thinking and feeling about troubled areas in their present lives and in their *own* childhoods; areas they perhaps thought had been laid to rest; areas they did not know were getting in the way of their being able to handle today's problems with their children.

"Suggested activities" include tasks that everyone can accomplish and that will help parents achieve immediate successes—and immediate healing. We all need successes in order to keep taking steps to deal with scary areas of life.

I have my own clients accomplish these tasks as we work together. I find that the combination of their exploring the problems on paper, and then experiencing concrete successes, is a powerful technique that gets a great deal done in a short time.

Helping professionals might want to avail themselves of the "Reflection/Action Guide" part of this book and use it to help give additional structure to therapy sessions. Many counselors who use my other books with similar guides tell me that this pre-structuring reduces the preparatory time they need to spend before each group session.

Parents, especially, have told me that they enjoy having this "extra hands-on of Toby" after each chapter. We're sort of "walking the walk" together.

SECTION ONE
FINDING THE RIGHT KIND OF HELP

ONE

THREE PARENTS
TELL THEIR STORIES

When parents hear other parents tell their stories of how it was, what happened, and how it is now; and hear them share their experience, strength, and hope with one another, their isolation is finally broken and replaced with a sense of wonderful new possibilities. That is why, in this chapter, I have not interrupted, with my own voice, the parents who are telling their stories to you. I believe that the healing power of their words exhibits the grace of God, passed from one parent to another.

Stephani's Story

"I was so scared that my kids would run off and die or that I'd lose their love if I said 'no' to them."

The first time I went to an alcohol/drug counseling session to see how to help my children, I felt overwhelmed with fears and anxieties. I found myself saying things out loud, like:

—How could I give my kids "consequences"? I had punished them *enough* by staying with their father, who is an alcoholic, and not having the courage to leave him. I felt it was "his example" that was leading them to destruction.

—I *know* I'm supposed to confront my kids about their drinking and drugging—but I *can't*. I'm too scared. And, on top of that fear, I feel so guilty about not doing what I know I should do for my kids.

—I feel I'm supposed to be a strong mother, and I'm not.

—I'm so scared of losing my kids' love. That's most of the reason I can't say anything to them.

—I'm so scared they'll run off, and get hurt or killed.

—I feel so sorry for my children. That's another reason I can't seem to say anything to them . . . it's like I think they almost have a right to drink or use drugs, to escape. It's so bad here at home.

—I feel so defenseless against alcoholism.

—I wouldn't even know where to start. Everybody in our house is so sick. I feel overwhelmed, most of the time.

I would tell my counselor, "I just can't stop crying and wringing my hands." And then the counselor would say, "Yes, that's exactly what you're doing. Now, what are you going to do about it?" And I would cry, because I *didn't* know what to do.

The counselor told me that behavior has consequences. I felt really mixed up around this issue. I couldn't punish my kids. I felt that their father, the alcoholic, was punishing them. That was punishment enough. I didn't know how to say no to those kids. I couldn't do anything about consequences. I felt guilty about my inability to act and the guilt only made me less able to perform. I was beginning to feel like a double failure—a failure as a parent, and a failure as a patient. But I was really too frightened right then to change any of my behavior.

Somehow, around this time, I went into Al-Anon. I began to see, through Al-Anon's gentle way, that when I did things, there were consequences. It wasn't punishment from God, but there were just consequences to behavior!

I needed about six months in Al-Anon, with its lack of expectations of me (I was *so* frightened), before I was even able to *start* to be an effective parent. I needed the undemanding support it gave me. People accepted me for what and where I was, at the time. Al-Anon never pushed me. It just showed me, through the growth of others, that there *was* hope for me, and for my kids.

The important message for me to hear was, "That's all right; you did the best you could. Just keep coming back." This approach gave me the time to work through my fears. No one blamed me for what I *wasn't* doing, or for not being at a point where *they* thought I should be.

I was given permission to take the time I needed, even though bad things were still happening and I wasn't doing anything about them. It took awhile, but eventually I was able to *face* what was happening. I think that's the crux of it . . . it's being *able* to face it. It's so hard for most of us, at first, especially those of us with an alcoholic spouse as well as addicted children. But even for those whose spouses are not addicted, it is hard for all of us to face it. We all need time.

"It was hard to say no to my kids"

I began to see that I had to say no to my kids. And that I wasn't being mean, or nasty, or making an extra burden for them. When I finally was able to see the results of their behavior—and see how their behavior was really hurting them *more* than they could be "hurt" by me saying no to them—then I was able to start to change.

Also, I thought I had to be strong to do all this. I didn't view myself as strong; I viewed myself as a wimp. It's like when they say it doesn't matter if you come into a recovery group to learn how to help someone else. It's okay if you don't start out to help yourself, as long as you *get* there. If you keep coming back, you eventually learn (everybody does) how to help yourself and what you can do to help someone else. You also learn what you are *unable* to do—what *no one* can do for someone else.

I began, slowly, to see that I had to do *my* part in helping my kids and family. And that meant saying no to drinking, drugging, and all the crazy behavior. Before, I felt that my kids almost *had* to have a crutch to deal with the pain of having to live with an alcoholic father. I knew what pain *I* was feeling . . . and *I* had Al-Anon! They didn't have *any* help. So, I believed that they had to escape through drinking and drugs.

"I began to see results"

When you keep going back to Al-Anon, or wherever you go for help, you begin to see results. It isn't abstract. You begin to have successes. That *is* what happens. I began to see that I should *not* put up with that kind of behavior. I began to see that I *could* risk my children's hate, and also that it's only a *temporary* hate. They are children and there are certain things you cannot permit; that's all there is to it. That realization

13

overrode the fear of losing their love or their leaving home. I had always been afraid they'd all run off, because that's what *I* wanted to do! I thought if I didn't have them at home, I'd have run long ago.

I started to think in terms of the future. Before, I had to focus on just getting through the day. There were so many crises then. My husband, and each kid, was acting out. Yet I had begun to get relief, even as the terrible behavior was still going on around me after I started saying no.

Somehow, I had absolute confidence that if I just kept going back to recovery meetings I would get the answers that I needed. And that's exactly what happened.

"I began to see my husband and children in perspective"

At a certain point, I moved away from my husband. When we were first separated, I thought he couldn't survive without me and that I couldn't survive without him. After about a month, I began to see that he and I were both still breathing so I knew it wasn't true that we couldn't go on without each other.

Once I was able to detach my emotions from my alcoholic husband, even a little bit, then other problems, like the children, came into view. I never was able to see them clearly before. There was too much else going on.

I also began to believe that I wasn't the cause of everything that was wrong, that I wasn't to blame for *everything*. Yes, I felt guilty that I had stayed with my husband for so long. But I was reminded that there were also outside influences on my children, and that they were individuals who certainly had free will. I began to feel like I wasn't so terrible. That I *had* done the best I could.

It was a hard realization. I had always wanted to make the family perfect. I strove for that, even when everything was so crazy. I guess I could not believe it was so bad. Once you go to get help, you eventually wake up. You "come to." You *see*.

What I saw, however dimly, was that something *had* to be done about my family, about my *crazy* family. Before, I kept feeling sorry for my alcoholic husband, for my kids, for me. Everybody feels sorry in an alcoholic home! And that's why nothing happens. You're afraid to *do* anything.

If I was going to make something happen, I realized that I was the one who had to believe in the rightness of what to do. It didn't matter

14

what anyone else said. You see, you can know in your head what's the right thing to do, but if you don't trust youself enough to go through with the plan, you're simply not going to go through with it. It's that simple.

Another important thing to realize is that other people—including children—have to become responsible. Even though they're your kids, and even though they've been deprived of one parent, or a decent atmosphere, and are ill-equipped to handle things, there comes a time when they *have* to become responsible. And that's the part where you begin to let go of your children properly, when you really begin to *know*, in your gut, that they must begin to become responsible.

When I finally began to see situations in terms of responsibility and consequences—that some things will happen or some things won't happen, as a result of my choices—I began to *know* what were appropriate things to do.

Consequences aren't *personal* to me. It's not like I'm *doing* something to someone. Before, parenting to me meant I had to punish. And I could not punish.

I was able to give my kids consequences when I was not able to give my husband consequences. With my kids, drinking became unacceptable behavior. I said, "You *cannot* drink; you *cannot* take drugs."

I began to see that my kids were in dangerous trouble, and that I had to do something. I thought of my husband as having the right to his own choices. With my kids, though, I became better able to say, "You will not do this." (That's what the counselors had been trying to teach me to do all along.)

I had thought I was defenseless against alcoholism. I thought our whole family was defenseless against alcoholism. I saw no hope. I felt that no matter what I did, my children were going to marry alcoholics or be alcoholics. Those odds were the most dreadful thing I learned in therapy. And then, to see it happening, was terrible.

From Al-Anon, I got another perspective: that in the end, it will all be well. I began to see that when one person starts treatment, the whole family begins to get well.

I was told that the worst thing is to do nothing. In the beginning, it was agony to read that in the Al-Anon literature, because I could do nothing! But I carried the hope that one day I would be able to do what needed to be done, because that is what happened to everyone else at

15

the recovery meetings.

"I allowed myself time to heal"

How did I allow myself time to heal, to get well enough to be able to make the necessary changes in my family, without the guilt that I was allowing precious, and maybe dangerous, time to go by? Since, in the beginning, I couldn't do anything anyway, I surrendered to that fact. I accepted it. I had no choice. I was doing my best that day. It was one day at a time.

I got my body to the recovery meetings, to prepare for the time when I *could* act. I found enough gentleness there, enough caring for me and enough acceptance—acceptance while I was crying, and immobile; acceptance with the knowledge that just because I was crying didn't mean the drinking was stopping. But people asked, "Was there anything you *could* do today? Were you able, emotionally, to do any more, today?" And I couldn't. So they told me that was my best. I was allowed to have my limitations at that moment.

When bad things happened to my kids and I was not yet able to do anything, I knew that in the end, if I did the best I could, that was the best.

When I told myself I should have exerted myself more, despite my fears and feeling immobile, I reminded myself that in order to *use* the program of recovery, in order to get *any* help, you have to surrender to the program. If you don't surrender, you're not going to be able to use the program. To me, my surrendering to it means I totally believe it—believe that I and my family can eventually get well. I accept that and believe it. And I have to start by accepting what I *cannot* do, today.

If I don't accept myself as I am, now, I cannot go forward. This idea allows me to start my day at any time. When you become aware that what you are doing is ineffective, you can start over, that minute. You can say to yourself, "Okay, this is not getting me anywhere."

"How my panic stopped"

Whenever I focused on *solutions*—what can I *do*—I got all screwed up. I'd get hooked into thinking the impossible, that if I "solved" the problem, then everything would be all wonderful. Or I'd scare myself out of taking any action because I was sure that it wouldn't work at all.

But I began to trust that even though there isn't necessarily one neat

16

solution, or one right way, there is help. I had great faith in reading things that I was certain would be helpful for me. That started making me feel very special. That maybe God *was* there. I would read something, and I'd go "Oh, yes!" So, help came in various ways, through a counselor, often people and my quiet times with God.

More and more, if you keep coming back to recovery groups, you're going to begin to have some serenity, which means you're going to begin to have some times when you feel *okay*. And it doesn't have to take years. I've seen it take just a few weeks or a few months. It's taken you a long time to get into this mess. So, you don't expect that in one day, everything is going to be solved. But you will begin to know that, ultimately, it's going to be okay. Your limitations will become fewer and fewer.

And at the same time, you learn to begin to be good to yourself because the program tells you to. You start feeling a little better. You gain some self-trust. You stop believing *everything* that *everybody* tells you, and you begin to discern. You learn to "take what you like and leave the rest," as they tell you in Al-Anon. You start to do that in life, with everyone.

There was a time when it felt as if I had ten counselors telling me to do something. The police, my husband (who was still drinking), everybody was telling me what the right "solution" was for my kids. And I was saying, "What *is* the right thing to do? I just *know* what to do."

As long as I retained the attitude that whatever intervention action I took about my child's alcoholism wasn't necessarily the final solution, but *another step*. I found some serenity. It kept the panic down.

"I found strength during crises and was able to intervene"
When my daughter was in the hospital, I learned to whittle down the problem. I learned not to worry about six months from now, when I was "sure" she'd be in trouble again. I learned not to worry about bills that *would* come up before they *did* come up. I learned to deal with what was in front of me right then. Before, it was all one big lump. That's why I couldn't do anything about anything. I couldn't sort it out. But I found I *could* do one thing at a time. I learned what to set aside for the moment.

When a crises comes and you're not in a recovery program, you just run in circles. But when a crisis comes and you are in a recovery program, you have a lot of practical options to choose from. All those steps that you've been hearing—how-to-get-better steps (and maybe you weren't practicing them because you weren't desperate)—they come back to you, then. Those things you "put on the shelf"—that before you couldn't do—they do come back to you. They do. You seem to make a conscious decision to try (even though you're scared) to do those steps. You *know* that you have to do something. When you come to a recovery program, you learn to trust that you will be given the answers, and you are. It just happens.

I said to myself, this is a process that has helped many people. Am I willing to *try?* It took the pressure off, thinking in terms of "I'll try," rather than "By God, it's going to work, or else!" I learned to see treatment as a process that would not necessarily fix my entire family all at once, but would begin the healing.

I tried to change my attitudes about intervention to see it as yet another step towards getting well rather than a fearsome "it-better-work-or-all-is-terrible" final solution. Once I learned to incorporate this more relaxed attitude about the *outcome* of intervention, I called a treatment center. Together with a counselor, I got my youngest two children, Sheila and Daryl, into treatment.

Stephani and I talked again, about eighteen months later. Her younger children were doing well. The older children (Kathy and Don, 20 and 22 years old, both in college) were still drinking. She was considering reuniting with her husband who had gone to a detox in Atlanta. He had been sober for five months.

Stephani *looked* different. Her hair, her posture, her eyes, all look more relaxed. The "wild, trapped animal look" she had before is gone. When bad days come, she *knows* they will pass. She laughs a lot more now, too.

She has no doubt that there will come a time when she will have the strength and the opportunity to nudge her oldest children toward treatment—but *her* sanity isn't dependent on that.

Laura's Story

*"I bought a whole library of books
on 'communication skills' and my child
kept getting worse."*

18

I raged to myself, "This is not happening! This child is my flesh and blood. This is my *life*. I raised him up in church. I gave him all the basics. This is not happening. This is just a stage he's going through. It's rebelliousness. I will *not* have to deal with this. This will just go away."

I ignored it for quite a while. He got worse.

Randy started drinking when he was eleven years old. Neither of us, his parents, were alcoholic. But, we were *both* adult children of alcoholics. My husband's father was an alcoholic. My mother was. I told myself, "This is the teenage phase. This is what the kids of today do."

The guilt was so overwhelming there was no way to alleviate it. I felt so *overwhelmed* I almost felt like *I* should take drugs. If it's my fault, I might as well be doing it, too.

I started to think that what would help would be my starting a whole new way of communicating with my son. I got ideas from reading books by psychologists on communication skills. I've got a whole library! I must have a hundred books, or better. I read everything I could get my hands on. If I saw an expert or a parent on a talk show, I made certain I went out and got the book. Nothing helped. My son was getting into more and stronger drugs.

So then I went to see a counselor. I got upset with what was happening because the psychologist thought we were dealing primarily with a *behavior problem*. He rarely addressed the drugs. When the psychologist suggested I give my son consequences for his behavior, what he meant was a consequence of punishment—not evaluation for a drug problem. He said that if my son stayed out all night, then he was to be grounded for three nights. Terrific. He could take drugs at home! And that's what he did. He smoked it at home.

When I explained this to the psychologist, he told me, "You have to take more control over your home." I took the television away; I took the telephone away. Nothing got better.

I was spending, on a sliding scale, seventy-five dollars a week to see this psychologist three times a week, for eighteen months. When my child got arrested because he started stealing to support his habit, the judge ordered me to see the same psychologist more often!

In group sessions run by this psychologist, I just got blamed that I wasn't tough enough, that the restrictions in our home weren't working because of me. That's when I started "counselor-hopping." I began looking for the "right" counselor.

19

I got to the point of wanting to jump off the nearest bridge. Then, thank God, something changed. I started going back to church—the right church. A church that understood.

The people I met there just listened to me. Nobody seemed to get tired of hearing my story over and over and over. I started feeling stronger. A few of them started to tell me to really get into attending Al-Anon and Nar-Anon, for parents of alcoholics and drug addicts.

I attended open meetings of Alcoholics Anonymous. A man came over to me after a meeting, and told me he had lost a son in a car accident. He said to me, "If your child dies out on the street, you have no control over it; but if he overdoses in your living room, you will die with him, over and over." That had an impact on me. It hit me like a lead balloon.

I realized that I *could* intervene. *I couldn't get him sober—but I could intervene.* What a wonderful, wonderful distinction. That distinction takes the pressure off parents to guarantee the results. And the pressure has to be taken off because you can't be in charge of results. It's impossible! All you can do is try. That's all.

At this point, I wanted to do an intervention but I also wanted to stop worrying about the outcome. I wanted to be able to let go of the results for my sanity! But I couldn't, even though I knew better, intellectually.

One Sunday, I went to church and the pastor preached directly to me. Afterward, he told me he had really prayed about this sermon and really wanted God to touch me and give me the wisdom and knowledge to know what I had to do with my child. So he delivered a sermon on letting go and letting God. He looked right at me during the sermon, and he said, "Laura, if you can, visualize this child on the altar and your giving God back His child and letting Him do with your son what needs to be done."

So, I visualized placing Randy right in the arms of Jesus and saying, "You gave him to me almost 17 years ago. He belonged to You then. He belongs back to You now. I will do whatever I can from this distance here, but he belongs to You."

The psychologists had kept pounding and pounding it into me that no matter what Randy did, I was at fault, even when he wasn't with me. Their solution was that I had to take control over him, over everything about him. But their real message was that he was not a separate human being.

20

But that Sunday, the minister was reinforcing for me the message that my son *was* a separate human being, and in his own right, a child of God. It meant that I could intervene and do what I could do as a parent who is responsible for trying to get help for my son. But I really saw that I wasn't in charge, or responsible for the *results*. I would do what God wanted me to do—as a tool. And if it was supposed to work, it would.

My minister was wonderfully supportive. He went through all the steps of the intervention with me. We set it up with an alcoholism treatment center and a specialist in intervention from that center. My son has been going to AA and NA ever since for two-and-a-half years.

Barbara's Story
"Back then, I had no courage."

I first went to Al-Anon because my husband was drinking and driving me crazy. The children weren't acting out, so I didn't think I had any problem with them. All I could see was their father—"the big problem." I kept thinking, *if* he was a good parent, *if* he wasn't drinking, *if* he was this, or *if* he was that. If, if, if!

I was in Al-Anon for three years before I was able to feel any calm while living there, to really detach from his behavior. Then, it seemed like the minute I was able to detach from him I started seeing the children's problems. Of course, I was three years along and the kids were older. I started seeing that Dana was drinking and doing drugs. And I knew the two youngest were drinking, though I didn't know they were drugging. But by then I did know enough to force them to go to Al-Ateen.

I wasn't thinking in terms of their needing treatment for their own use of alcohol and drugs. I felt they were just getting solace for themselves. I thought their "acting out" was their way of dealing with their father's drinking. It didn't occur to me that they had drinking problems! Even though I would say the words, "The majority of kids whose parent is alcoholic, become alcoholics or marry alcoholics," the implication was just too scary to contemplate because I was still dealing with their father.

But they truly could not bear going to Al-Ateen. And I could not bear to put them through one more thing. So, after about three times of herding them into the car and dragging them to a meeting, I didn't try it anymore.

One day, my oldest child, Mimi, told me that her father had threatened her with a gun. The kids said, "You've got to do something" and I said, "I can't, he's sick." I felt that that was a turning point for them; they felt they could no longer depend on me. It was terrible.

But I was beginning to peek at the frightening questions: What was I *really* getting out of this? Why were he and I together? What was so important about our staying together?

He wasn't coming home and I was miserable most of the time, but I still clung to those few little good times and thought they were enough. I just couldn't bear even the thought of leaving. I really believed that if I kept going to those recovery meetings, somehow, magically, I don't know how, I was going to be able to affect the children in a totally positive way. Somehow, I would be able to counteract *all* the mess.

Now, I think, "Why that's preposterous!" There's no way I could stop *all* the damage. There's no way one person can undo a whole family disease. I could set an example of how to get well, but I couldn't zap them all well.

But going to Al-Anon did do something. I think it set an example. I think they saw me grow, gradually getting well. And, I do recall the kids did watch me. They would kind of look at me to see what I was going to do.

You know how the alcoholic has contempt for you if you're being wishy-washy? The kids were that way with me. If I would give in to their father over something, the kids would be kind of snide. They were a lot more openly angry with their father. I had covered *my* anger over the layers of denial and rationalizations.

For a long time, I felt abandoned by my kids. But I kept thinking that if I could only get myself well, I could somehow help them. Not that day, and maybe not that year, but somehow I was going to be able to do something, and it wasn't going to be horrible. The situation wasn't hopeless. I really did believe that I could get well. And I believed that if I placed my kids in God's hands, they too could get well. But the idea of actively pushing them to treatment—I couldn't do it for the longest time.

Today, it would be different. I would *insist* that they get some kind of alcoholism treatment much sooner. There wouldn't be any two ways

22

about it.

Back then, I had no courage. I couldn't accept that I had to do what I had to do, and they could feel however they wanted about it. I was always so worried about their feelings, I ended up doing nothing, which made it worse. I was so afraid of offending.

As they watched me change and get well, I remember that when I did things in a *begging* way, Mimi had a "look." She was contemptuous. But when I began to say no and show some strength and simply said, "Do not argue, just do it!" she admired me.

I got her respect. I think I never realized you had to earn it. It's not that you always have to be strong, I learned. You just have to *be* a parent. It was a very wonderful time for both of us. I was flexing my muscles, as a parent, and I was more sure of myself. And because *I* was sure, *she* could relax a little.

I was beginning to find some peace of mind even while I was still struggling to learn how to be the parent I wanted to be. I began to realize that, first of all, it's never too late. If I had looked at the whole mess all at one time, I'd have said, "Oh my God, I've got to do *all* this!" I'd have probably shot myself. But by then, I had been going to recovery meetings long enough to have seen myself grow some. I had learned that I wasn't all-powerful. My children were going to do things, separate from me, whether or not I was a good parent. They were going to do things on their own. By that time, I saw my job as a parent was to give them leadership. I couldn't do it *for* them, but I could give them some choices. I could teach them that actions have consequences. That was one of the most important things for me.

Slowly, I began to lose my guilt. Slowly, I got the strength to look at what was really going on, to face the problem. By then I must have been a little well, or I wouldn't have been able to.

When you face something, you talk about it. It's no longer a hidden secret; it's no longer mysterious. Then you're just ready to do. I think when you're ready to accept reality, you get to a place where you accept your own humanity; you accept that you can't control or fix everything; you accept that it's not all your fault. You stop focusing on whose "fault" it is, because that's not the issue. You begin to focus on getting you and your family well, one step at a time.

At first I felt guilty when I stopped feeling so bad. But, I knew I was doing the right thing. Feelings aren't facts. My disease was always saying, "Why are you happy when you're in this mess?" It would tell me, "Who are you kidding? It's whistling in the dark." But I knew it wasn't. I don't know how, but I just knew I was on the right track. I think it helps to have successes.

And you do have them when you stay in a recovery program. You absolutely have them. You feel different; you look different. You have renewed hope. It's almost as if you automatically do the right thing. And when I say "right thing," I mean the appropriate things around the disease of alcoholism. Now, you don't get that overnight, certainly. But you get reinforcement every time you go for help. If one person in that family gets well, it's going to change the dynamics of that family.

I felt much more guilt detaching from the children's problem than from my husband. The children *were* my responsibility. But I got over the guilt. It's the old "sick and tired of being sick and tired" routine. I've had too many good days—and I wanted more.

I didn't want to live that old, sick, worrying way. Even though it felt very normal to worry! You get permission, in the recovery meetings, to let go of guilt. At the same time, you're getting tired of it. You see, you can't take as much guilt as you used to, because it isn't justified any more. The whole idea is that you're a person and that you have a right to your own existence. That was a revelation to me. I never was a person. I was always somebody's wife, mother, kid. I had never grown up.

I began to get some adult perspective. I stopped looking for immediate solutions—the I-must-do-it-by-four-o'clock syndrome. Al-Anon's idea of detaching from the problem has something very relaxing about it. It's knowing that if I stay as intensely involved in this problem as I am now, I'm going to be entirely ineffective and unwise, because I'm nuts!

Detachment is learning to pull fifty percent of ourselves out of the situation. The fifty percent we pull back is to calm us down; it's a pulling-back to get sanity.

We get very rigid. We get rigid in our quest for the perfect answer. We ask not only "Did I say the right thing?" and "Did I have the right tone?" but "Was my *motive* good?" The motive thing will drive you nuts.

That's our disease talking. In recovery meetings we learn that the goal is healthiness, feeling good. It doesn't matter how you do it, the purpose is to feel the least uncomfortable. Sometimes it's the choice between two uncomfortable paths.

And if you backslide again and again, so what? Very few people go straight into what's good for them. For most people it's a zig-zag, from a point where you don't do what's good for you to a point where you do, moving back-and-forth and forward at the same time.

Perfectionism can tear your insides out. Recovery is a gradual, imperfect process. That means you don't go to treatment for six months and then suddenly get well and know how to make the right decisions. There's a lot of back-and-forth, and back-and-forth, which really is good because it's a way of "backing in" to what's good for you.

Every time a repeat situation arose it was like a new situation. It was like I couldn't *learn* from my experience. I couldn't trust my instincts. I kept doubting myself. I was too rigid. In order to make a move, I had to go through all that learning mess again. But, in time, the self trust comes.

I was doing everything I could and I began to believe that it was inevitable that the kids were going to do things that were sick. But I went ahead and made plans instead of sitting home and waiting for the things to happen. Because they were going to happen. I wasn't projecting; I just knew that Dana who's been in and out of treatment was still sick. But I'm not losing sleep over it. The one worry that I have in the back of my head is that she'll die. But I can't live like that. I've sort of accepted that if she doesn't accept help, then it's a possibility she'll die.

Mimi's doing okay, though. Now that she is out on her own, is married, and has a child, she's begun to look to the future, and in the process she has begun to clear up the past. She started going to meetings for adult children of alcoholics six months ago and has been attending twice a week ever since. I have a lot of hope that Dana can get well too.

And I have intervened with Dana a lot to get her help. So I've done what I could. It's a matter of whether I can let go of the debilitating worry. And when I'm not able to, I simply pick up the phone and talk with the counselor who has some contact with her. The last time I called, the counselor said, "I told you if anything should happen, I will let you know." I said, "Well, I know if something bad happens, you'll let me know. What I need is reassurance today. I'm very anxious, right now. I just want to know if you've seen her." She said she'd seen her and that she seemed okay. That was what I needed.

25

Al-Anon teaches detachment with love. When you first start detaching, you don't feel like it's love, believe me. because your idea of love is worrying. So, you're going to feel terrible when you begin to not worry. You might not even feel love; you might feel hate. Don't wait for "detachment with love" because you don't know what love is anyway, when you first come to treatment. And don't wait until you're strong enough to do something.

Reflection/Action Guide

Write On:

1. Remember and reflect on a casual comment made by a friend or colleague (who did not know that your child has a drinking/other-drug problem) that resulted in your retreating more into silence because you felt such shame.

2. If this is the first time that you ever read or heard a parent tell exactly what their fears and guilt were, write down your emotional reactions to this revelation.

3. Write the phrases or sentences that you may have heard from counselors, friends, family, that increased your fears or guilt. See if they coincide with what made Stephani, Laura and Barbara fearful, and how they got past those fears.

Suggested Activities

1. Start a small notebook; write the phrases that give you comfort from this book. Keep this notebook with you at all times.

2. If you haven't attended Al-Anon, allow yourself to go to a few meetings to see if you can avail yourself of the wonderful gentle help there.

3. Begin to think about seeing a counselor who is a specialist in families of alcoholics. The hotline page in back of this book is a good place to call for referrals.

4. If you are too afraid to go to a counselor or Al-Anon, at this point, put the idea on the shelf, and allow yourself to come back to it later.

TWO

IS IT JUST A PHASE?

Most parents of teenagers in the 1980s are in their late thirties and forties. Back in the 1960s, marijuana and psychedelics were just making their way on to college campuses and avant-garde high schools, especially on the East and West Coasts. But who knew much about cocaine or valium? Who had ever heard of teen alcoholism and cross-addiction? And who could imagine ten-, eleven-, or twelve-year olds experimenting with PCP and other "designer" drugs?

What are you hearing today from educators? From the media? For the most part you are hearing very confusing, frightening, and alarmist generalities and pronouncements. But what is *really* important is sorting out the right information—and the correct information—and knowing what it means in terms of *your* child.

Can "responsible" kids become alcoholics?

The major educational focus today is on alcohol and drugs as an issue of moral integrity, a matter of "being responsible."

What is dangerous about that perspective is that kids can reach age twenty-one, can legally drink alcohol, can do so in a "responsible" manner—*and can still become alcoholics.*

This strength of character approach does not at all consider that we

29

are talking about a *disease*. When children who come from the sixty-percent of American households which have a family history of alcoholism use addictive drugs *at all* (and that includes alcohol, which is a drug), they are at a *very* high risk of developing an addiction.

A further danger of this strength of character approach is one I have not heard spoken about at all: If we continue to view teen addiction as merely a usage problem and if we see the solution *only* lying in kids' abstinence, we are not facing the untreated family problems that are a direct result of family members' lives revolving for years around a chemically-addicted person. Once a kid has stopped his or her usage, we want to believe that "the problem is over."

Even many parents who are members of community-advocacy groups working to stop drug problems balk at going to Al-Anon! A majority of these parents have addicted children or are themselves adult children of alcoholics. Yet they often do not view alcoholism as a disease, but rather as an issue of will-power or moral choice. Hence they see no need to go to Al-Anon.

We must stop seeing ourselves and our children as either strong survivors who can say no, or weak people who got hooked. Otherwise, not only will we not get over the effects of this family disease, but we will be reinforcing the centuries-old mistaken attitude toward alcoholism: that it is solely a matter of strength of character, or moral integrity, of right and wrong.

I know too many ministers, priests, rabbis, nuns, and other very good people who drank with very "responsible" attitudes, *and still became addicted.* For that is the nature of the disease (as we'll see in chapter three dealing with the genetic facts about alcoholism). Your body can either metabolize alcohol, or it can't. If it can't, and if you drink *any* alcohol, the addiction process will set in—*regardless of whether or not you drink responsibly.* The more we perpetuate the idea that alcoholism is a question of moral integrity, the more alcoholic adults and children and their families will be reluctant to go to treatment. Who wants to appear weak? Who can bear the social stigma?

Facts on teen addiction

No matter what other drugs a kid may try, if he or she tries *any,* alcohol is very probably going to be one of them.

When there is a history of alcoholism in your family, even if your child "just tries" alcohol (or any other addictive drug), there is a very high chance of the addiction process being started. Your child can "just drink on weekends at parties" and the physical addiction can begin.

Once that addiction process begins, cross-addiction is a complicating, dangerous element that needs to be considered. Cross-addiction means that once the addictive process starts, no matter what addictive drug your child ingests (and that includes "just beer" or "just one joint"), the addiction is kept active, and progresses.

Now, we come to the "synergistic" factor. If more than one addictive substance is ingested, a multiplier effect takes place. In practical terms, this means that if an adult takes one valium and has one beer, the effect is equal to drinking about ten beers. But we are not talking about the addiction going on in adult bodies—but in children whose livers aren't yet fully developed.

There's a *5-to-15 rule* commonly used among teen-addiction specialists: On the average, it takes 5 to 15 years for an adult male who drinks, but who does not take other drugs as well, to develop a chemical addiction. (A combination of alcohol and other drugs speeds up this process tremendously.) On the average, it takes 5 to 15 *months* for an *adolescent*, and 5 to 15 *weeks* for a pre-adolescent.

So, when I'm asked, "How can he be an alcoholic—he's so young?", the answer is horribly simple to explain.

The four most significant causes of death in 16- to 24-year-olds are all *directly* alcohol or drug related: auto accidents, suicide, homicide, and drug overdose.

Sixty-five percent of the children of alcoholics become alcoholics or marry alcoholics.

Ninety percent of teenage alcoholics go on, often after an apparent lull in drinking, to become adult alcoholics unless they get help from alcoholism treatment centers.

The progression of the illness of addiction, whether alcohol or other-drug related, is never a straight line. You should anticipate periods where there is more usage followed by less usage. This is the period that fools most parents. They believe the "less usage" of beer, or wine, or pot, or whatever, means the child has the addiction under control.

Facing the addiction *is* less painful than denying it

Parents I talk with almost invariably express the understandable hope that their children are "just going through a phase"; that is, drinking as a result of going through a "teenage psychosis," rather than seeing the craziness as a *result* of alcohol or drug abuse. They hope it is "just a phase" because they want to believe that if they ignore it, eventually it will pass.

When parents tell me that their children are calming down a bit and seem to be getting their lives in order, I hesitate before I plunge in and remind them that 90 percent of the time, we're dealing with a disease that will not "just go away."

I hesitate because I know what the reaction will be. There will be a confusion in the face, a clouding in the eye. Typically a mother will look away from me in a second or two of terrible panic, before brushing her hands in front of her face as if brushing away the idea. Then she will change the subject.

As a counselor, I know that I must remind parents of reality. But I feel their pain. "It was almost unbearable!" they are saying. "Why bring it up again?"

Yet if I don't, I'm lying. I would be helping parents pretend that if the drinking isn't going on now, it won't go on again later. But it often will. If I pretend it won't—and help perpetuate the idea that it won't—then, when the alcoholism raises its ugly head again, the parents will spend more time denying what's happening because of me, and will spend more time in pain.

Why does denial equal pain?

I absolutely believe that once parents have spent some time in Al-Anon or addictions counseling, and some healing has taken place, then it is easier to go through the acute pain of facing the alcoholism than the chronic, horrible pain of not facing reality and experiencing the relentless guilt, confusion, bewilderment, and augmented pain that we all feel when we do nothing.

Why do I say that the acute pain of facing the alcoholism will be over with quicker if we face it, than if we deny it?

Because, after counseling thousands of members of alcoholic

families, I have found that after the first step in confronting the disease is taken the other steps are easier—*much* easier. It *always* looks harder before you do it! Plus, the self-respect parents feel when they finally do something that they know is good for their child is enormously comforting.

What if your child seems to be doing better?
If your child is not showing symptoms for a while (that is, he or she is not drinking, or is "controlling" the drinking), why not believe that it might be "just a phase" and *not* alcoholism?

Well, it is possible that your child is getting smarter at hiding it, so you are finding out less about what's really going on. It may be that you are understandably exhausted and want to find out less. And it may be that although your child is "getting it together" (meaning, for example, getting good enough grades in high school so he or she will be supported financially while in college), he or she might just be "biding time" until the proverbial escape away from home and parental control where circumstances allow your child to do what he or she wants to do, including a lot of "partying."

It may be that the disease is in one of its "remission" stages, and you can breathe easier, but it's not usually a good idea to think it's all over.

Parents, learn to be gentle with yourselves
Oh, the ways parents beat themselves. They want to know what is going on and they feel they have a *right* to know. But even when parents recognize that alcoholism is a disease, still they partly believe the lie that they are "butting in"—and partly they are afraid to find out the truth.

If you are like most parents, you are so scared you feel immobilized. You've probably read the "tough" articles that tell parents what they are supposed to do, no matter what they feel, "because it is the job of parents." No one, it seems, is talking about your concerns, except in a dismissive way: "Sure you feel terrified, but that's part of being a parent. So, pull up your socks, and do what's right for your kid. Otherwise, what kind of parent are you, anyway?"

Remember how scared you were as a new parent? Remember how you bought Dr. Spock and other childcare books? Remember how you read everything you could find in order to figure out what that cough

33

meant, what that rash meant? Please try to read the list of symptoms that follows in the same way. These symptoms only indicate the beginning of a disease that is so arrestable, so treatable, that the only shame is to ignore the symptoms.

A little pain and a little panic to get a child to treatment is nothing compared to the joy of recovery. And your child will be grateful to you when he or she is truly sober. *I know you can't believe that now!* It's the cunningness of the disease that makes *everyone* in a family believe the *disease* when it bullies parents and tells them they'd better "butt out!" The *disease* is trying to scare you into thinking you'll lose your child if you just dare to look at it and see the symptoms your child might have.

Now, if you can, read the list of symptoms that follows. Stop when you want to. Come back to it when you want. There is to be no shame, on your part, about being afraid. All of us have these fears. That's part of the nature of the family affliction aspect of the disease. Only family treatment, in Al-Anon or another parent self-help or professional group, works for most people in finally getting rid of these disease fears.

If the list that follows is too scary for you to consider, just allow yourself to put it on the shelf, so to speak, to perhaps think about later. This is very important—no one has the right to push you into thinking or doing what you are not ready for. Later, when you've attended Al-Anon or a parent group for a time, and feel supported enough, calm enough (no one is calm around this stuff; I never feel that one has to be calm in order to make a decision, nor do I feel that one gets rid of all doubts before taking action), then re-read this section in order to be able to determine the actuality of the situation.

Thirty symptoms of addiction*

1. Has your child stayed out all night, without your permission? (Before you say, "All kids do that," they *don't* all do that.)

---

*NOTE: This list has been compiled with the aid of top experts in the field of adolescent addiction. It is not an exhaustive list, however. Parents and therapists may note other symptoms that could indicate a pattern of addiction in children and teenagers.

2. Have you come across inappropriate things in his or her bedroom?

3. When your child comes home, do his or her eyes look bad?

4. Does your child come home seeming "spaced out"?

5. Does this child physically hurt younger brothers and sisters?

6. Does your child act up at public gatherings where a certain decorum is expected, and where other kids are behaving properly?

7. Has a teacher or principal called you about your son or daughter?

8. Has he or she been suspended from school?

9. Are this child's school grades worse than they were last year?

10. Is he or she truant?

11. Has your child dropped out of sports or other school activities? Does he not want to lift weights when he used to? Did she used to like tennis, and now makes excuses not to play?

12. Has there been a change in your child's dress, even within the implied dress code of his or her peers?

13. Does your child no longer do chores willingly, if he or she used to? Are you given as an excuse, "I have to go out"?

14. Does your child tell you, often, that he or she "has to meet friends on the playground?" Often, in elementary or junior high school, after hours, the school grounds are filled with alcohol and other drugs. Parents tell themselves, "I'm glad my kid is straightening out and going along with school friends to play." (After all, when *we* were kids, there *weren't* drugs on the playground.) And you, of course, want to believe your children. We think it's a moral issue; we forget it's a disease.

15. Does your child refer to "pleasurable" drinking that is months or years in the future? ("I can't wait to go to college so I can drink and party there!") Or, if you're talking about another person who stopped drinking, does your child exclaim, "But, what about beer and crabs next July?" (when it's now December).

16. Has your child ever come in after a good time and commented that he or she drank everyone under the table?

17. Does your child use the word "party" as a verb, rather than as the noun that it is? (i.e., If your daughter is going to an upcoming party, does she talk about "partying" in general, or is she talking about the *people* who might be there?)

18. Does your child want to spend the night at a friend's house often? Does Susie's mother maybe not mind if they drink "just beer"? Does your child tell you that Susie's mother will be there, and she's not? Check on the facts.

19. Are you finding empty liquor or beer bottles under your child's bed?

20. Is your child hanging out at a shopping center? Is there a liquor store there? Are the kids buying booze there, or getting an adult to buy it for them?

21. Has your child's circle of friends changed in a way that is noticeable?

22. Are drugs in the medicine cabinet slowly disappearing? Kids often get their initial supply of drugs there.

23. If you keep alcohol in the house, does it sleem diluted? If you've had a party, have people claimed that it seems weaker than usual?

24. When you ask your child questions, does he or she seem to "skate"; meaning, not being direct with answers, but kind of going all around the point, being vague?

25. Is money missing from your pocketbook? From piggy-banks in the home?

26. Is your child getting an allowance and lunch money, and still coming back and saying he or she needs more?

27. Are your possessions disappearing?

28. Has your child been stopped or arrested by the police for drinking while driving?

29. Have you ever considered seeing a professional about your child's behavior?

30. Has your child ever spoken about, or attempted, suicide?

If your child has two or three or more of these symptoms, they often form a pattern of *probable* addiction. Children manifest these symptoms differently, at different timcs. As discussed earlier, at times they may appear to stop altogether. That is the disease's deception which makes parents think that their child's problem is gone, that it has cleared up.

AA says that alcoholism is cunning, baffling, and powerful. So how can you know—when the symptoms disappear for a while—if the problem might really be gone? Well, unfortunately, the statistics are not on your child's side. The disease may lie dormant, by the seeming "controlling" of it, and your child may appear to "do well" again at school and in general behavior. But, if that child holds on to his or her "right" to drink socially, *that* is often a symptom of a continuing problem with alcohol.

Suppose you had always enjoyed strawberries and had no problem eating them. And then one day you ate some and got violently ill. If the doctor said you'd probably have the same reaction sometime again if you continued to eat them, you would gladly pass them up in the future. You wouldn't have a problem letting go of strawberries, except occasionally, when they might look especially good. However, just remembering your illness would make you shudder and say no thanks.

Only an alcoholic will fight for his "right" to drink and argue that it's no problem when it is. Why is it so important to fight for this right? Your child doesn't know it, but it is his or her biochemical craving that's doing it. The disease is telling your child's brain to argue you under the table, to humiliate you, to bewilder you when you try to help so that the alcoholic can continue to drink.

But alcoholism is not an indictment of your parenting skills. A child who drinks does not tell you to "butt out" because you're a bad parent, but because the *alcoholism is talking*.

Reflection/Action Guide

Write On:

1. What do you tell yourself when you begin to see a possible pattern of addiction in your child?

2. What are the "reasons" you give for your child's addiction patterns, other than the fact that they are symptoms of addiction?

3. Write out the ways you have been taught to not "see" addiction when it is there.

Suggested Activities

1. When you begin to fear reality, pamper yourself *immediately.*

2. Remind yourself that we family members make molehills out of mountains.

3. Allow yourself to re-read this chapter when your child's alcoholism acts up again.

THREE

PARENTS ARE NOT GUILTY: THE GENETIC FACTS ABOUT ALCOHOLISM

Nothing is more immobilizing or more terrorizing to parents than the guilt they experience because they feel that they somehow caused the alcohol affliction in their children. Mothers tell themselves, "I should have left her father," or "I should have stayed with them." Fathers say, "I should have paid more attention," or "Maybe I was too hard on them."

Even parents who have been in specialized family alcoholism treatment programs experience this guilt. They may say it's a disease without believing that deep down.

Parents who have been in Al-Anon, sometimes for years, often believe that the term "family disease" refers to the family rather than the disease. They believe that if their children get alcoholism too, it is because of the *example* set by the drinking behavior of family members rather than the result of an inherited physical tendency.

NOTE: Parents, show this chapter (and also the Chapter, "Young AA Members Anonymously Talk About Suicide and Other Issues") to your children. They may be more willing to listen to the facts from a neutral "third party" than from their "unreasonable" parents.

41

If your guilt is based on a belief that this disease is caused merely by bad parenting, it will be greatly diminished when you understand and accept the true *physical* nature of alcoholism.

Dr. James Milam is the author of *Under the Influence* and co-founder of the Milam Recovery Centers in Bothell, Washington. He has been a pioneer in the United States in educating mental-health professionals about alcoholism as a primary disease. I asked Dr. Milam how parents can determine if alcoholism is in their family.

He immediately stated that psychological and social problems do not cause or even contribute to being an alcoholic. Then he went on to explain that we've got genetic material from two parents, four grandparents, eight great grandparents, and so on. All that genetic material combines in a lot of different ways. In genetics, it's always a matter of probabilities. Rates of alcoholism in different families range from near zero up to near 100 percent.

I asked, "So people who say that it is not in the family are not looking very far back, when they're talking family history?"

He said, "Right, and there are several reasons why, if they do look back, alcoholics are missed in the family tally. Until very recently, alcoholism was almost never diagnosed as alcoholism. Because of the shame and stigma, parents almost never told their children that a grandparent or a great grandparent, or anyone else in the family, was a drunk. Denial has a long history.

"Then, too, in counting alcoholics in the family, it's important not to overlook the total abstainers. The reason people abstain is nearly always because of their own alcoholism or their reaction to their parents' alcoholism."

I thought about this. In most families, no one would ever admit that a grandmother could have been an alcoholic. But a good way to determine if this were so is to find out if her adult children were teetotalers. As Dr. Milam said, almost all total abstainers do so as a revulsion-reaction to parental alcoholism.

And there often are many other hidden women alcoholics in family histories as well as uncounted early-stage alcoholics, who even today, are rarely recognized. Most people can only see the disease when it is very obvious, when the person is in late-stage daily maintenance drinking.

I have heard countless parents tell stories of "Uncle John" or

"Cousin Smith" who died in an accident—"and, yes, he drank a lot, but no one thought he was an alcoholic!"—only to discover months later, when they had finally tracked down the family rumors, that the uncle or cousin had been thrown out of the house years earlier until the drinking was finally brought under control and the family went back to living as usual.

Suppose you want to see if alcoholism is in *your* family. "Statistically," Dr. Milam explained, "if you want to see how heavy the predisposition might be in your children, you have to see how many people out of a hundred, on both sides, have alcoholism in your family. That means, in order to get a large enough sample, you've got to look a lot further back than grandparents! Most people, when saying that they don't have a family history of alcoholism, don't realize that they have to look back about six or more generations to see if the predisposition is ten percent, or twenty percent, or more, in their particular family history."

A number of scientific studies have explored this hereditary phenomenon, Dr. Milam explained, and have proven that alcoholism *is* genetic. First he talked about the well-known "foster-home study." Scientists studied adults who had been separated from their biological parents at birth and raised in foster homes. These adult children had no contact with or knowledge of their birth-parents. The study of participants were divided into two groups, and their alcoholism rates compared. One group had biological parents who were known to be alcoholic; the other (the control group) were from biological parents known *not* to be alcoholic. Twenty-five to thirty percent of the adult children of the alcoholic parents were found to be alcoholic; in contrast, the alcoholism rate of the control group was only about five percent!

Dr. Milam told of an opposite kind of study which confirms the finding that heredity, not environment, is the prime cause of alcoholism. The children of non-alcoholic biological parents who were raised by drinking alcoholic foster parents were no more likely to be alcoholic themselves than if they had been raised by non-alcoholic foster parents!

This research doesn't deny or minimize the psychological trauma and devastation of being raised by drinking alcoholic parents; it just says that the environment isn't what *caused* their children to grow up to be alcoholic.

Thousands of research studies over many years have tried to link up early psychological problems with later alcoholism. *All* have failed to find *any* such connection.

Another remarkable and very well-known study was conducted by Dr. George Vailliant of Harvard University over a forty-year period in the Boston area. In 1940, some 600 young men, half from college and half from town, were studied for personality, character, family history, school records, community relations, and other factors. For the next forty years, the study participants were reevaluated every five years to see how earlier experiences affected their lives. During the course of the study, the alcoholics were identified.

In 1980, all the data was correlated. The researchers looked for early-life experiences that would explain why some of the men became alcoholics and why others did not. To their surprise, the researchers found that except for heredity, nothing else correlated!

This result meant that in Dr. Milam's words, "All of our favorite reasons for developing alcoholism went out the window: poverty, serious family problems, delinquency, poor self-image, antisocial personality, depression, mental illness, stress on the job or at home, the lack of financial success. *None* of these had anything to do with who was alcoholic!"

But what *is* it that gets inherited? What *is* it that makes this disease "genetic"?

"We already know many things that are different about alcoholics *before they even start drinking*," states Dr. Milam. These are differences in brain wave patterns, in how they metabolize alcohol, in nerve transmitters, in blood sugar management, and other differences in how the liver and brain process and react to alcohol. And recent reports indicate that researchers have identified the alcoholic chromosome and are working to identify its specific genetic components."

It's not over and done with

Parents know their kids are crazy while they're on booze and drugs. But once they're sober and clean and have been through treatment, parents often ask, "Why do they still need to go to all those AA meetings afterwards?" These parents may have let go of (at least some of) their guilt about having caused their children's alcoholism. But

44

they may have replaced it with the idea that "genetic" means the alcoholism is just a physical disease and stops just as soon as the actual drinking and drugging stops.

But alcoholics, including children-alcoholics, cannot be cured. Alcoholism is a disease that can only be arrested, one day at a time. The triggering mechanisms are always there and can be set off with a drink or other addictive drug, even after fifteen years of abstinence. Alcoholics need AA to remind them that they *are* alcoholics and cannot drink, because the disease is patient and will wait until a person's guard is let down and there is no mental defense against the first drink.

Newly-sober alcoholics, of any age, go through what is called the "protracted withdrawal syndrome," which can mean up to thirty-six months of withdrawal symptoms, including anxiety, mood swings, depression, and unknown fears. The amount and intensity of these symptoms will vary with the person and with the amount of alcohol or drugs that are stored in the system. Some drugs take more time to leave the body, because they are not water-soluble and are stored in the fatty tissues.

When alcoholics are going through this withdrawal of chemicals from the body and brain—experiencing the fears, terror, and depression—very often, *only* the reassurance from other recovering adults and teenagers who have gotten through this period can convince your child that these symptoms will truly pass; that he or she need not fear the symptoms; that one *can* get through it without drinking or using other drugs. Remember, your child has a long-time habit to unlearn: the habit of getting immediate gratification for emotional pain, of not waiting for it to pass, or believing that it ever will pass. You might be thinking, "Oh, my child only drank for eighteen months before we got him to treatment." That may be so, but eighteen months is a big chunk out of a young person's life. The learning process has definitely set in, and must be unlearned.

So you see, even though this disease is physically *caused,* the mental and spiritual effects of its onslaught are enormous. Stoppages, breakages, "short circuiting" in the central nervous system and brain affect vital areas, including those that make or distort decisions about basic life values, and whether or how to attain them. In a child, this is particularly precarious, since his or her value system hasn't even

45

gotten a chance to fully develop.

For alcoholics, once usage has stopped and the chemicals have been withdrawn, much reparation to the body and brain must be made. Dysfunctional patterns must be unlearned. I believe that AA's Twelve Step program is the best reparations system going.

In the same sense, after the usage has been stopped, parents, too, need reparations done to them. Kids need to make amends to their families as AA says, to help restore family balance. This does not mean that kids are guilty. They've been sick, not bad.

Here's an analogy: Suppose I had undiagnosed (and therefore uncontrolled) epilepsy and, in seizure, I fell and broke a neighbor's lamp. No, I am not guilty, but the lamp is still broken. In all good conscience, without beating on myself that I was bad, I still need to replace the lamp. For my own peace of mind, I cannot ignore the unconscious guilt I would be inviting on myself if I knew that damage was done (even though by accident) but I didn't care enough about my neighbor's feelings to help right the issue. With this perspective, I would need to make amends. So too, I need to right wronged relationships while maintaining my dignity.

After the usage has been stopped, parents need to make amends to themselves, too. They need to seek help in Al-Anon or a family recovery group to help *them* to recover from the terrible guilt, rage, worry, and resentment that has been perpetrated on them by this disease. These symptoms (especially the resentment) do not just go away overnight.

Going to a family recovery group that specializes in parents whose children are actively addicted or recovering addicts does *not* mean that it is the parents' fault or problem. It means that the parents have intelligently chosen an effective way to more quickly get past *their* symptoms of the disease. To go it alone can prolong the recovery for years.

46

Reflection/Action Guide

Write On:

1. Write out a future day's scenario where you see yourself rational and guilt-free about your child's illness.

2. Start writing a family-alcoholism tree, an investigative project to free yourself from the family-disease symptom of irrational guilt.

3. Write a list of phrases you've told yourself that make you feel as if you contributed to your child's addiction.

4. Now, write the factual answers to that list.

Suggested Activities

1. Every time you're about to chastise yourself for "having done" or "not having done" something that "might have set the scene" for your child's addiction, re-read this chapter.

2. The very next time you feel guilty, tell yourself to stop, and say, "That guilt is *my* disease talking!"

FOUR

WHY MOST THERAPIES HAVEN'T BEEN ABLE TO HELP

Since many parents have gone to clergy, counselors, and general mental-health practitioners, and have become even more confused and despairing after doing so, this chapter is meant to clarify why the sessions may have been ineffective and why your kids' problems often got worse rather than better during the course of the therapy.

This chapter will be a beginning in helping you to make better choices about choosing counselors for your children, your spouses, and yourselves.

This chapter also will be helpful to the ever-growing number of therapists who are recognizing how pervasive all forms of alcoholism are in their caseloads, and are looking for addiction education and understanding to add to their expertise and enhance their effectiveness.

What are the basic myths all of us have been taught about therapy—myths that *prevent* the healing of alcoholic families, myths that do not take into account the disease concept of alcoholism and all that it implies?

Myth #1: Patients always tell therapists the truth about their drinking.

I have spoken with thousands of parents who took their children to see a therapist in an effort to bring some sanity back into their households. After the therapist posed a question or two to the child about his or her drinking, the matter was often dropped. Why? Let's look at a typical encounter:

Therapist: Do you drink?
    Child: Yeah, some.
Therapist: How much?
    Child: A couple of beers, at parties, with other kids. That's all. All the kids do it. My mother's paranoid.
Therapist: Why do you say that?
    Child: I don't know. Ever since we moved, after my father got transferred on his job, my mom is really unhappy. She takes it out on all of us. My dad's always telling her she nags.
Therapist: Does she?
    Child: Yeah! Ask my sister if you don't believe me. She's going to leave home as soon as she's eighteen next year. She told me she can't stand it there any more.
Therapist: Do you feel the same way?
    Child: Yeah.
Therapist: Let's talk about that, next session. Maybe we can find some ways for you to talk more directly to your mother about how you feel about the way she treats you.

This therapist has made her first mistake by believing the alcoholic's minimizing of the drinking problem. The child's disease helped him divert the issue completely.

Alcoholics—even child alcoholics—will lie to protect their drinking. In counseling, I've never had an alcoholic patient tell me that he or she drinks more than "a couple." Alcoholics are incapable of telling the truth due to a disease process that is extremely cunning in its efforts to protect its supply of alcohol. This is not a moral judgment. It is merely a fact of the disease. (See the list of questions at the end of this chapter to ask yourselves in order to crack through much of the child's denial and get at the truth. If you find a family history of alcoholism and if your child seems to have a problem, too, chances are your child does have a problem.)

50

If your child's therapy sessions proceed from the first myth—that your child told the truth about his drinking—then the next logical conclusion in this erroneous thought process is to think that, instead of addiction being the problem, "underlying mental-health issues" must be to blame.

Myth #2: These "underlying mental-health issues" can be resolved by teaching "good communications skills" to members of that alcoholic family.

This is impossible. Your alcoholic child can be very sincere and really want to cooperate by trying to communicate better. But even after a terrific family therapy session, all his insight can go flying out the window with the next intake of alcohol. Furthermore, every day your child continues to drink, the disease is progressing. That means that in addition to experiencing secondary physical problems, his or her ability to cope with life at all is progressively diminished.

If your child is going through withdrawal, the severe agitation will be causing anger, anxiety, and overall, an inability to have *any* "good communications."

Myth #3: Alcoholism is a result of unresolved conflicts, anxieties, and undealt with anger. As soon as your child and therapist can "get at the root of the problem," the need to drink will wither away by itself.

I have personally seen terrible results from belief in this myth: Early deaths of children that could have been prevented; much confusion and despair for families; and the waste of lots of time and money in ineffective treatment sessions.

Putting it simply, *problems* do not cause alcoholism. Almost all of the time, after alcoholics stop drinking and attend AA regularly, their serious emotional problems disappear or at least diminish greatly with help. On the other hand, it is *impossible* for the still-drinking alcoholic to get well emotionally.

Myth #4: Even if the alcoholism is not dealt with as the primary issue, good therapy is being practiced if families are straight about feelings.

Even during therapy sessions where the alcoholic *is* acknowledged

51

to be an alcoholic, many therapists have been trained to focus on asking parents how they *feel* about all this. On the surface, this may seem sensitive and caring. Unfortunately, such an approach often leads to fifteen, thirty, or even fifty sessions on how each family member "feels about" everybody else, and not much else is accomplished.

In this erroneous process, the next step for the therapist is to help everybody to improve their communications skills about how they feel! By that time, the drinking is no longer brought up on any regular basis. The drinking is merely discussed in terms of how everyone else feels about it.

When feelings—rather than drinking or drugging—are in the spotlight, then the onus is on parents to justify their over-reactive feelings (say, when their child may stop drinking for two or three weeks) and does not take into account the dynamic of the child's addiction and the constant tensions and crises it perpetrates on you.

More damaging, perhaps, is the probability that your therapist can get sucked into believing the charming facade that even an alcoholic child is capable of producing, thereby invalidating the credibility of your statements (that it *is* crazy, living in that household). The therapist thinks the alcoholism may be being exaggerated.

Myth #5: The alcoholic does not know how the family feels.

I'm also skeptical of counseling methods that assume your child does not know how you feel! It does not take three months of therapy sessions with Susie (who's constantly truant from school) to let her know that her father and mother are angry!

Counselors *wish* that if parents stated their feelings and needs in a straightforward manner (that is, learned "good communication skills" in order to "express feelings appropriately"), then the child would be given the incentive needed to want to stop the drinking or drugging. Not only is this magical thinking, resulting from lack of knowledge about the dynamics of the disease process of alcoholism, but it again subtly places the responsibility for the cause of the drinking on the parents, instead of on the alcoholism. (Parents often quit the counseling at this point, feeling even more depressed and despairing than when they entered counseling!)

I believe there is at least a partial explanation for this lack of understanding and knowledge about the disease concept of alcoholism. We all once believed alcoholism's lie that "the alcoholic wouldn't drink if all was right with his or her world." Unfortunately, no one's world can be just right.

Another partial explanation for this professional lack of knowledge about the disease concept of alcoholism is more hidden: many helping professionals are themselves adult children of alcoholics, spouses or former spouses of alcoholics, and parents of addicts. Since denial is the main symptom of alcoholism and addiction—and since professionals are no more immune to this symptom than anyone else—when counselors are themselves untreated for their family disease symptoms, they bring this denial symptom to their work. Thus, we have a client whose main problem is a disease that may remain undiagnosed because the therapist's own family disease remains undiagnosed, because the therapist's main symptom, too, is denial around even *seeing* the disease!

Myth #6: When parents are told they are "enablers," it leads them to stop the enabling.

"Enabling" is meant to describe the rescue operations that the spouse or parent of an alcoholic carries out, when he can't stand watching the alcoholic suffer the consequences of the disease. When that happens, he "cleans up" the alcoholic's messes (lies to the school that his son has the flu when the child was actually picked up for drunk driving). That way, the alcoholic doesn't suffer the real consequences of his behavior.

A parent must learn, eventually, to get some detachment on watching these crises happen in order to stop cleaning up after the child. The idea is to allow the *disease* to hurt the child so much that he or she wants to get sober. Of course, it takes a parent a lot of time in a healing group such as Al-Anon in order to be able to do this. And this detachment can't be forced or rushed by counselors. It is a slow process, and very frightening.

When a mother rescues her alcoholic child and I label her an enabler, she obviously is still doing the rescuing behaviors and is not yet unafraid enough to give them up. She knows I am being judgmental when I use this term. Even when I say it lovingly, I seem to be admonishing her to go faster than she is capable of doing at that time. And she feels despairing, because she *is* doing her best. She may get so discouraged and frustrated and overwhelmed that she stops treatment.

More specifically, the term enabler implies that while the parents did not *cause* the drinking, their rescue operations *contributed* to the perpetuation of the drinking. Such thinking is dangerous; it leads alcoholics, who are *already* looking for a way to blame others for the drinking, into again placing responsibility for the drinking on the family.

Alcoholics do not need any encouragement to blame others! Alcoholism counselors spend most of their time trying to crack through the blame-systems of alcoholics. It is considered to be a major breakthrough in the wellness process of alcoholics when they begin to acknowledge that *nothing* "got them drunk." In contrast, alcoholics who have had relapses and are re-entering treatment are now often heard saying, "I wouldn't have gone out that time if I hadn't been enabled!"

The alternative to being labelled enablers is to teach you to end the rescue operations through the simple but effective process of detachment. For, detachment will help end your fears—and it is your fears that originally caused you to rescue. And even though, in this book, we are primarily talking about parents and kids, the detachment process is especially important if you also are married to an alcoholic. It is important for you to lose your fears of that adult alcoholic so you can get on with your life and become more able to deal with your children-alcoholics.

How does detachment work? How does it help you to lose your fears of your alcoholic child or spouse? The general process goes something like this:

1. When you begin to learn ways to stop watching the alcoholic in order to begin the healing process of seeing to your *own* needs, the alcoholic has radar and senses this switch in focus.
2. Much of the "games" stop then, because the alcoholic child knows that less attention will be paid to him or her.
3. By continuing to focus on yourself instead of the alcoholic, you get an even greater distance (detachment) from the threats, and begin to lose your fears of them. You begin to see how you gave

the alcoholic so much of his or her power. You can take it back!

4. Again, the alcoholic senses this. He or she begins to threaten even less.

5. You *see* that detachment works! You gain more confidence. Many of the illusions in your household are beginning to end.

6. You lose much of your preoccupation with the alcoholic. Your preoccupation was based on your needing to stop him or her from hurting you. You now see they are much less capable of hurting you than you thought. They've already done most of the damage they can do. But the game has been to keep up more of the same junk, to keep up the *illusion* that the alcoholic is powerful. This no longer works. You have learned to not look at him or her; to walk out of the room; out of the house—to not beg.

7. The alcoholic now stands alone with his or her disease. They've lost their audience, and therefore drop much of the bullying. You are not watching it.

8. The alcoholic can no longer get you to believe you are responsible for his or her drinking and for the craziness in that house.

9. The alcoholic has a chance to grow up and make a decision to get help.

10. You are free.

When I teach parents the dynamic of what I have just described, they begin to naturally let go of the disease—to detach, and therefore stop enabling—because they are losing their fears of the alcoholics. All of us stop manipulating and controlling people when we lose our fears of them.

As a therapist, I try to let parents know that I will gently help them along the not-straight road toward freedom from their fears. I let them know that they do not have to meet a timetable. In fact, I let them know that I am aware that I do not walk in their shoes, that *they* must be comfortable to make even a small step; that what I will do is love and accept them, even when they vacillate in their ability to detach from the disease.

I let the parents know that I know they will be ready some day. I try to give them the same hope that Al-Anon holds out—that my acceptance of them will be part of the healing and will help move them along toward health and the choices that they now can only dream of.

And then, gently, naturally, interventions *do* happen, because with one hand I provide the healing embrace and comfort of total acceptance and without pressure; while with the other hand, I hold up the mirror of reality and nudge them along ever so gently toward reality.

Is There a Family-History of Addiction or Alcoholism?

Twenty questions for family members. Answering yes to any two of these often indicates alcoholism. Ask these questions about yourself, your spouse, parent, grandparent, uncle, aunt, sibling, cousin, and any other family member.

Have/do you or the other relative . . .
1. Ever talked about switching from liquor to wine or beer?
2. Have idiopathic epilepsy?
3. Have adult onset diabetes?
4. Have essential hypertension?
5. Ever complain or "nag" about a relative's drinking?
6. Have adult children who are teetotalers?
7. Did anyone ever talk about a relative's drinking?

Did that relative . . .
8. Seem to drink a bit too much?
9. Fall a lot?
10. Fall asleep on the sofa a lot?
11. Have a lot of arguments?
12. Seem to be able to drink more than most people and not feel it?
13. Have any liver problems?
14. Go from job to job?
15. Have credit problems?
16. Ever get stopped for drunk or reckless driving? Or ever have a single-vehicle accident on a weekend night?

17. Frequently have a red nose? Red eyes?
18. Have a beer belly?
19. Seem to be either the life of the party or a loner?
20. At the mention of alcoholism, bristle and get defensive, or abruptly leave the room?

Reflection/Action Guide

Write On:

1. Describe how you may have needed an Al-Anon meeting to recover from a family therapy session.

2. Describe the ways you believed your ineffective communications with your child caused the addiction.

3. Describe your feelings when you read or hear that you are an enabler.

4. Using the process of detachment just described, visualize a scenario in which you can see yourself no longer reacting to the alcoholic in one of the situations you find chronically troublesome.

Suggested Activities:

1. Make a list of family members who were probably alcoholic (use the twenty questions as a guide).

2. If your current therapy is not addressing the alcohol or drugs as the primary problem, consider getting a second opinion or evaluation for your child at an alcoholism treatment center.

3. Turn to the hotline page in the back of this book, and make a call to a treatment center and ask for a brochure to be sent to you.

FIVE

SUICIDE, THERAPY, AND OTHER TEEN ISSUES: YOUNG AA MEMBERS (ANONYMOUSLY) TELL THEIR STORIES

We've heard parents talk about their struggles to face the disease of alcoholism and help their kids. We've heard Dr. Milam talk about alcoholism being a primary, cross-generational disease—not a result of "mental problems" or "poor communications." We've seen through some of the myths common to family treatment and looked at some effective approaches for healing the family and moving the alcoholic toward recovery. Now let's hear recovering teenagers and young adults tell us how they see it.

I interviewed a group of young people in AA whose sobriety ranged from one year to over ten years. As a professional observer, I've attended many open-to-the-public young people's AA meetings. I've noticed that a surprisingly large number of young people who speak at these meetings recount episodes where they attempted suicide. These stories touch on parents' deepest fears—fears about their own child dying, or about the death of another child by an accident. So my questions focused on this frightening issue as well as on other topics that arose. Their answers reflected their age and experience. During the discussion I found myself constantly amazed—their depth of honesty was awesome.

Toby: Did you ever contemplate suicide? Attempt it? Were you drinking or taking other drugs at the time? Were you in withdrawal—needing alcohol at that time, instead of drinking? Did you believe, and did your parents believe, that the drinking was a result of emotional problems?

Steve: (Five-feet-eleven, blond, relatively newly sober, spoke first): I just turned 21. I started drinking young. When I was drunk, I got really depressed. The drunker I got, the more thoughts of suicide would enter my mind. I can remember trying to drink myself to death. I figured if I got drunk enough, I could get my breathing down to where I wouldn't wake up.

I had lots of car accidents and pretty bad injuries. I always got drunk, blacked out, and wrecked the car. My parents decided they'd have more control over me if I was made to stay home, as punishment. So, I just drank at home. Then they started seeing how much I really drank. My father kept saying, "There's something wrong with that boy. He's crazy!"

And, man, did I ever give the impression that I *was* crazy! At the drop of a hat, I'd be off in another world, or violently breaking something up, or just being very distant. When I was seventeen they couldn't take it anymore, so they sent me to a psychologist.

Toby: Were you asked about your drinking?

Steve: Not at first. One day, I remember her specifically asking me, "Do you drink?" And I said, "Yeah." And she asked, "How much?" And I said, "Oh, a beer once in a while." Then she asked me, "Do you smoke pot?" And I said, "Once in a while." And that was that. Occasionally, she'd comment that I looked high, but I was really drunk. She assumed that since I was so young, I'd be on drugs. But I was drinking.

Toby: Were you ever *confronted* by her about your drinking or smoking pot? Was it ever discussed in terms of, "That's probably your problem?"

Steve: No. As a matter of fact, just the opposite. She told my parents that it was all a matter of "family difficulties." She said we had a problem with our "family unit." And recommended that we *all* go for therapy. I went for the better part of my junior year of high school. My mother went every week. My brother went every week. And once a month, there was a get-together for the whole family.

Toby: Do you know how much this cost?

Steve: It was all the same every week: $60 an hour for me; $60 for my mother; $60 for my brother; and then, $60 for all of us together every month. About $800 every month.

Toby: Did your suicidal thoughts let up while you were in therapy?

Steve: The one actual attempt I had was *while* I was in therapy. No one, *no one*, connected it to my increased drinking.

Toby: Have you felt suicidal at all since you got sober?

Steve: Early in treatment. When I was in withdrawal and needing the stuff. I thought I was going out of my mind. Then, when it got out of my system, not since then at all. Not even the thoughts.

Toby: What about you, Talbot?

Talbot: (A little older, serious-looking, with a quick smile): It was always during a blackout, when I drove my car into a reservoir, when I hit bridge abutments. I started to realize that my drinking was somehow related to the bad things that were happening, but by the time I realized it, I didn't care.

I didn't actually tell myself I didn't care. It was just in the attitude I carried about everything. I didn't like the world; I didn't like myself; I didn't like anything. My only friend was escape.

NOTE: I've found in my interviews with young recovered alcoholics in AA that many had exhibited a pattern of attempting suicide, not necessarily when or because "problems" got worse, or because the adolescent didn't have someone to talk things over with, but because they had reached the stage in addiction when the alcohol or drugs lost the power to deaden pain. I think this is terribly important to look at, because lately, we hear at school and in the media that alcohol was *a factor* in a suicide attempt, but only one; and that it could have been prevented by better, more attentive communications with the child. In certain cases, this may be so. But I think that *many* more times, we need to look at the addiction involved as the *primary cause of the suicidal thinking.* We need to recognize the fact that most addicts, at some point, reach a stage of terrible despair when the alcohol or drugs no longer provide the escape from emotional pain that they once did—that the alcohol or drugs actually cause and *increase* the pain. The addiction *must* be detected and treated despite the child's denial, if further suicide attempts are to be avoided.

63

I've watched other kids. I've been sober over ten years. I must have been to over 7,000 young people's AA meetings. I hear lots of kids talking about when they were suicidal. They just didn't know any other way out. It got to a point where the booze and drugs just didn't work, anymore.

Toby: Why don't you say more about that.

Talbot: I think that with most people who are alcoholic, booze and drugs are a fantastic reliever of everything. You feel great, you feel euphoric, nothing's wrong in your life. The more we drink, the more we want more of that good feeling; we can't get enough. But after you get into the later stages of addiction, it doesn't give you the same effect. Even when we drink a gallon, half the time we *can't* get that effect. It has stopped working.

It no longer helps us escape from the pain of reality. It has made that pain worse. We haven't learned how to cope in the first place, and then it no longer takes the edge off. Sometimes, we do get to that plateau, but it's short-lived and then it's over.

That's when a lot of the kids get into what I call the serious-attempts suicide stage. The alcohol doesn't work anymore to get them out of the depression they're in—the depression that is made so much worse *in the first place*, by the alcohol.

Steve: I was a full-blown alcoholic in late stages by the time I was seventeen. But, when I hit my senior year in high school, I used all my willpower to control my drinking, so that my parents would think it was all over, and they'd pay for college, and I'd get away! Then I could do what I wanted.

I blamed all my troubles on the fact that I was stuck in a small town. My parents were wonderful so I couldn't really blame them. But I did, in a way. I said they were too strict. That's because they got mad when I drank!

But, my disease was patient. When I got to college, I drank all I wanted, because no one was watching or yelling at me.

Josh: (His young, sweet, freckled face belies his years of suffering): My therapist and my parents were *sure* my problem wasn't drugs or alcohol. None of them saw what I drank. I

64

lied; I was charming; I got good grades. *That's* what is wrong, they thought: I was too bright! I was bored!

My brother's an alcoholic, too. They thought he drugged because he had learning disabilities. I guess they didn't think about the kids who had learning disabilities who *didn't* drink.

Toby: Suzie, did you believe, when you saw yourself as a burgeoning actress, that drinking was adding to the romanticism of all this? Did you see yourself as "an artistic soul" who needed this edge-of-life thing that alcohol could do for you?

Suzie: (Round-faced, adorable, an actress and a young woman who did not look like anyone's stereotype of an alcoholic): Actually, as a result of my drinking, I literally tossed my opportunities aside. I'd get these big shots at doing things, and when it came time to do them, I was worthless. I had a policy that I'd never drink right before an audition, or right before a show. But, the problem was that I didn't see that I was still hung-over from the night before. And, if I hadn't had a drink in three days, I *needed* one. It was a no-win situation.

Toby: Did you think you couldn't be sober and also be really passionate about the arts?

Suzie: I found that the passion for acting—serious acting—was there even more *after* sobriety. Because I had my priorities straight! I've done my best work sober, and I've been told so by people who didn't even know that I was an active alcoholic. I think it was an illusion I created, that this liquid gave me courage.

Jim: (A quiet, shy youngster, who has difficulty speaking in a group): A friend of mine who I drank with and went to school with was a football player. He had this drive, this obsession you're talking about. He pursued football with the same kind of feverish hunger that you did with the acting. The "all-or-nothing." He thought he couldn't play unless he was drinking.

Talbot: I tried to play football in high school, and I was lousy. I used to get drunk over that. I'd get drunk and play football. I thought I could play when I was drunk!

Steve: I knew, eventually, that I was an alcoholic. That is, I knew I needed alcohol. What I *didn't* realize was that my life was such a wreck *because* of alcohol. I thought I just needed alcohol because my life was a wreck. I had it backwards.

I was drinking in a bar, and this bartender just got disgusted with me. I was so young, and he said, "Steve, there's something wrong with you." He threw me out of the bar. Then, he took my keys and asked me, "What do you want me to do with you?" I had been to AA and remembered people talking about treatment, about emergency detox. So, I told him to take me to detox. He drove me around all night, looking for a detox that had a bed open. Because he knew I needed help. I was just beaten. It was just like it finally dawned on me, I'm going to die, I'm going insane, I can't take this anymore. The next thing I knew, I had an I.V. in my arm. The doctor asked, "Do you think you have a problem with alcohol?" and I said, "Yes, I do."

Reflection/Action Guide

Write On:

1. If you are a parent, describe how this chapter may have helped you feel even more confident about proceeding with alcohol or drug treatment for your child.

2. If you are a helping professional, describe how this chapter may be helping you to focus the thrust of your therapy in a different direction.

3. If you are a teenager, describe how you may find yourself identifying with any of the kids in this chapter.

Suggested Activities

1. Parents, when you become fearful of your children, re-read this chapter.

2. If you have not done so, show this chapter to your children. If you have, show it to them again another time.

3. If your therapist seems surprised by the information in this chapter, perhaps you should consider seeing someone who is a specialist in dealing with children and addictions.

SECTION TWO
THE TREATMENT PROCESS

SIX

INTERVENTION

Parents' real feelings about intervention:
Is it always a loving process?

Intervention usually is described as a loving process. However, I hesitate to use the word loving because of the guilt it induces in a great number of parents.

Yes, of course, parents love their children. And in most cases, a loving intervention is easier to accomplish with a child than with a spouse. In many spouse interventions, so many years of bitter feelings have passed that there needs to be much post-sobriety rebuilding of the marriage before real love can glisten through again.

However, even with a child intervention, most parents are *very* angry. And understandably so. At the very least, parents feel betrayed. "How could you have done this to us," they wonder, "we who gave you love and everything else?" Usually, parents are sick and tired of being lied to, stolen from, financially drained, yelled at, cursed at, and emotionally battered.

Even when parents know, intellectually, that it is okay to have these feelings of anger, most often they still feel guilty. Parents assume they should feel unconditional love and harbor no ill feelings toward their child—especially when they learn that this son or daughter has a disease and was not just wantonly bad. So even though intervention *is* a truly loving process, many parents, when hearing the term love, hear an indictment of their angry feelings, and further proof of their failure as parents.

Other parents find comfort in knowing that this process is loving. Indeed, they find that the only way they can follow through with an intervention is to remember that it *is* one of the highest forms of love they can give their children.

Most parents experience a combination of both reactions. As a counselor, I need to continually remind them that love feelings are absolutely not necessary in this process and that anger and even feelings of hate are totally normal given what they have been through. Parents, too, have a right to feelings! But when guilt replaces anger, I try to immediately respond by reminding the parents of the very wonderful thing they are doing for their children. Much of my counseling process during the weeks preceding the intervention goes from one of these reassurances to the other, over and over, back and forth, until the parents can complete the intervention. While the child is in treatment, other issues come up, but this dance between guilt and rage crops up repeatedly.

Much of my role as a counselor is to provide the hope that these feelings will subside (and they always do); and to be patient while parents work through the same guilt-and-rage ground, over and over.

Often, this paralyzing emotional seesaw absorbs all the family's attention and keeps the parents from clearly seeing the child's manipulative behavior. The payoff in helping the parents, of course, is that they end the mood swinging and recover from their years of anguish. The children recover faster, too. When Mom and Dad stop putting all their energy into a seesaw that always remains on the same spot, they are able to take new steps on their own, and their child's behalf.

Besides the guilt and anger, most parents I've worked with share other common fears. Extremely common and very understandable, is a fear of the unknown: that is, fear about what treatment centers are and whether they are bad places for children and adolescents. Other parents who have been in Al-Anon are afraid that their very shaky sense of detachment will lessen instead of grow during the intervention process.

72

"I'm afraid to send my child away."

Dr. Gerald Shulman, Vice President of Addiction Recovery Corp., and a nationally renowned expert in adolescent addictions, told me in an interview, "Parents need to be told that they're doing the right thing, that they are not bad parents. Parents need to hear that their guilt and fear and anxiety are felt by other people in the same set of circumstances. They need to know that the counselors will do the best things for them and for their children, that they are in the corner *with* them."

Dr. Shulman explained that when parents phone for information, they often are afraid to say that they are calling about *their* child. They often begin by asking him general questions about adolescents and addictions. "Do you treat adolescents?" is a common starter. Or they say they are looking for help for a friend. Often, at that point, they are scared of any personal involvement.

Dr. Shulman will provide general information, he will reassure the caller that the treatment center is not a medieval dungeon with bars and guards, and he will talk about how he and his staff are experienced professionals in the area of alcoholism and drug addiction. One he's laid the groundwork, he'll say, "We're talking about *your* children, aren't we?" Usually he hears yes. He goes on to reassure the parents that he certainly won't hurt the child, and almost always can greatly help. He invites them to tour the center and talk to the kids there.

When, out of fear, parents back away again and say, "Oh my God, what am I doing calling you!" Dr. Shulman answers, "You're calling me because your child has been threatened with expulsion from school or because he's stealing from you and looking and acting crazy or he's taken the car without permission. You're calling because the behavior will most likely get worse—because you want your child to be safe."

Most parents who call a treatment center already know their child has a problem. What they are really saying is, "Help *me* to feel okay!"

"I'm scared that I'll get hooked into even more craziness."

Another barrier to parents doing interventions is their fear and confusion around the "right" attitude toward intervention. Many Al-Anon members hesitate to do interventions because they believe the process will embroil them further with the alcoholic. Very rightly, they want to *detach* from the disease, not get more enmeshed in it!

I believe a good intervention process *does* accomplish this detachment. A good analogy is a job intervention with an adult. The boss simply tells the alcoholic that he'd better learn to fit in with the scheme of things as they are at the office if he wants to keep his job. The employer does not change the world of work to fit the alcoholic; the alcoholic must get sober and meet the demands of the job.

In the same way, parents don't have to fit into the sick scheme of the child's disease any longer. In an intervention, they are saying to the child: "The drinking and drug use must stop. You must get help, get sober, stay sober, and fit in as a member of the family."

Good family counseling with addictions specialists helps parents lessen the fears and guilt they experience when they demand that their children begin acting responsibly. I find that parents need tremendous reassurance and support around this issue because they are so used to getting hooked into their child's guilt-tripping.

"I'm not sure I'm ready to do an intervention."

At this point many parents can feel almost ready about pursuing intervention and treatment options, but are bewildered about where or how to begin. The following suggestions should be helpful. Be sure to tailor them to your needs and particular situation at this time.

First of all, go to Al-Anon. It is extremely effective whether or not you also attend professional therapy and specialized parent groups. You will need support for yourself while going through an intervention, or, if you are not yet ready, you will need support while you get prepared. Additionally, you will need further support during the time your child is in treatment, and after he or she comes home.

Next, if you can emotionally do it now, begin looking for a treatment center for your child. There are many listed on the hotline page in this book. Use the list of "Questions to Ask a Treatment Center" at the end of this chapter as a guide when making inquiries over the phone. While most treatment centers provide excellent care with excellent results, it's important to be an educated consumer even in a time of crisis. Make sure the center you're considering has the experience, programs, and philosophy that is right for you. At the very least, choose a center that is AA oriented.

Make a decision about whether your child needs to go to a nearby center or one further away. Take *your* needs into account, too. If you are feeling distant and hostile towards each other, maybe a breather

74

away from each other is good. If your child is very young, or dependent on you, a close place might be better. In either situation, try to find a center that specializes in kids.

Ask the center you call if they have a family therapy group for parents. Explore the group. If you are not ready to set up an intervention for your child, tell them, and see if they have a group that will allow you time to explore the issue and get ready. If not, call another center.

If you are not yet wanting to participate in a parent group or do an intervention, you might want to just tour a center. Allow yourself the right to be emotionally just where you are.

You may want to begin individual (instead of group) counseling, for any number of reasons: privacy, or perhaps a full hour for just you. If you're attending Al-Anon, you may be getting enough group experience but you may also want a more intense, focused time on your particular situation. Many of the treatment centers listed on the hotline page can refer you to a counselor in your area that specializes in kids and addictions, and who will understand your needs. Also, some people seem to speed up their recovery a bit by attending Al-Anon, a professionally led group, and going to individual counseling.

You'll find the right combination of treatment and intervention options by testing, exploring, and allowing yourself to be true to your inner needs. Remember, do not be intimidated and stay in counseling or any group where you are uncomfortable. Also, you might find that as your situation and your child's situation changes, you will go on to other settings that meet your needs.

"Is a specialized adolescent program necessary?"

Adele and Hyman are parents of Stephan, a fifteen-year-old who's been using alcohol, pot, and cocaine for three years. They had written out their questions before they called me, concerned that they might leave something out. They wanted to be sure that they chose a center that met all their needs.

"We haven't yet investigated, Toby, but suppose we find there isn't an adolescent center close enough to make us comfortable?" they asked.

"Well," I advised, "make sure the adult center that is closer is AA oriented, has a good follow-up program for Stephan after he leaves there, insists that he attend AA nightly once he's out and that he gets a good AA sponsor. You'll also want to find a center that has a supportive and gentle family program for the two of you."

Usually, though, I feel better when parents choose an adolescent center for their kids, even if it is further away. Children at an adult center are sometimes doted on. They may be treated as a "mascot," especially if the center is not used to having very young people as patients. That kind of attention is not good for an alcoholic who must learn, as part of the wellness process, to become less attention getting.

In an adolescent center, many things are different from an adult center:

- The length of stay is more extended because rather than going through an adult process of "rehabilitation," adolescents must learn how to get "habilitated" in the first place. Also, going home too soon can mean getting back into a powerful and potentially destructive peer group situation before the habit of sobriety is well established.

- Classroom instruction or tutors are provided to compensate for missed time at school.

- Gyms are common since kids have so much more energy to work off than do adults.

- Counselors are child-oriented. They know that the worries of a teen are much different from the worries of an adult. (An adult male worries whether his wife will leave him; a child worries that he has a pimple on his nose.)

- Treatment centers teach kids about responsibility, often for the first time in their lives. Most of them have no track record of being responsible to anything or anyone. At a center, the kids are told that if they don't come to group on time or if they don't make their beds, they lose privileges. If they have a food fight, they are told to clean the unit.

Many treatment centers are developing adolescent programs and opening up additional facilities. If you have looked for such a center in past years, you may find that many new options are available, and much closer by.

Steps of the Intervention

1. Ask yourself if you are ready.
Remember these facts:
- —It's one day at a time. If you are not ready today, you just might be tomorrow or next week if you are attending a recovery program for the families of alcoholics.
- —You do not have to be fearless or without doubt in order to proceed. Almost no one goes into an intervention without fears and doubts, even knowing the facts that ninety percent and more of interventions are totally successful!

2. Make sure you have "clout."
Ask yourself:
- —Is your child young enough for you to have legal control?
- —Does your child have an arrest record? (You can enlist the aid of his or her probation officer to do much of the intervention.)
- —Does your child's school have a student intervention program? (If so, cooperate with them and let them do the actual confronting *for* you.)
- —If your child is of age, is there something that he or she wants from you very badly? (College tuition? The use of the car? Perhaps you employ your child in a job he likes and wants to keep?)

3. You can intervene with one child at a time.
Remember these facts:
- —You can pick the easiest child to do an intervention with first, if more than one of your children are addicted to alcohol or other drugs. This can enable you to see that it's not as difficult as you thought it would be. We always are more scared of the unknown. When your child leaves treatment and is sober and attending AA meetings, there will be *two* of you in that household with clear heads and you will be able to help each other with the others.
- —If your spouse or parent also is alcoholic, you may find it easier to intervene with that adult before you begin to think of intervening with your child. Give yourself permission to do

what is easier first.

—It all seems very overwhelming. Remember that no one is standing behind you with a gun and with a schedule! Remember also, after one intervention is accomplished, the parent often doesn't even have to do another! It's like the domino effect: one child pressures another, in a way that no parent can do. The change in the house is great after two people are sober—and miracles often happen "by themselves."

4. Go to Al-Anon. This is an intervention, too.

When you attend meetings and learn the tools to give back the disease to the alcoholic, you are helping to isolate the disease from the rest of the family. And you are allowing the alcoholic to begin to grow up and choose sobriety. When despairing parents tell me of older children who they've "tried everything with" (including treatment), and they say they're at their wits end, and "feel like failures," I tell them that attending Al-Anon *is* "doing something more."

This "something more" is turning it over to a Higher Power who can do for us what we can no longer do for ourselves. I believe my Higher Power knows when I've tried my best and can no longer "do."

One of AA's "twelve promises" is that "we will learn that God is doing for us what we could not do for ourselves." Many times, after we've done what we can, and then "let go," it all works out.

5. Choose your professional who will lead you through the intervention.

Begin, if you wish, with the hotline page in this book. Also see the local telephone directory in your city; especially the display ads of treatment centers that focus on the *disease*. Remember that *you* are paying. *You* are the consumer. If someone doesn't strike you just right, go on to the next one. Choose an interventionist you really "click" with.

6. Choose the right people to be involved.

Choose the family members, friends, school personnel, job

personnel, friends, that have relevance and clout with the alcoholic, to be part of this effort. Arrange a date for when everyone can be there.

7. Write out the facts.
Document the events and your feelings about them to present at the intervention. Go back a few years and gather your data.

8. Time it right.
Choose a time when the intervention is a surprise, at a time when you know your child will be there (7 a.m. often is a time when you *know* your child will be home).

9. Do a rehearsal.
Everyone will rehearse to see that it *is* a factual process and that you can leave the leading of it up to the professional. You'll learn to stick to the facts that you've written down. This takes much of the unpredictability out of it and does not allow the alcoholic to divert you. Each person will read the facts about how the behavior has affected him.

10. Bring in additional documentation.
For persons who cannot be at the intervention, but who wish to participate, get their letters, tapes, even a video of them lovingly urging the afflicted alcoholic to accept help. This can be powerful, especially if the person is important to your child.

11. Choose the treatment facility.
After you've read this book through, you will probably have the kind of facility in mind you'd like. Talk this over with the interventionist. If he or she is employed by a specific treatment facility, you may not be able to work with her or him and have your child go elsewhere. This is not a problem if you feel good about the interventionist and good about the center. Check out both.

12. "Suppose it doesn't work?"
This is always the fear of the family. Fortunately, the statistics

show that almost all interventions work out well. Even if the child refuses treatment at first, often, within a week, he will go in anyway. Or, in some cases, when the child is very, very fearful, he agrees to attend AA on a regular basis without going to a treatment center first. Isn't that wonderful? I tell parents who are afraid to go through with intervention because of the wrath of the child, that if the disease is allowed to go on, unchecked, it is progressive and fatal. And the child's negative feelings will increase if you do not intervene due to the progression of the disease.

13. Now we enter the intervention.

You've gathered together all the people who are important to your child; all of you have written down the facts of the disease and how it has affected all of you; you've chosen your intervention specialist and the treatment center; you've rehearsed and read what you've written down.

Your child comes downstairs or into the house, and you tell him that there are some people who want to talk with him in the living room. Perhaps you mention that John, his favorite person in the world, is in there too.

14. Hand it over to the interventionist.

As your child enters the room, you introduce him to the interventionist, who then takes over, much to your relief. He explains to your child that everyone there loves him and cares about him very much. He says that they all have something to tell him. He then goes around the room, and all read the five or six things they have written down about the child's behavior while he was under the influence that have made them feel bad. Your child will try to interrupt, but the interventionist will calm the child down, letting him know that he will have a chance to speak, too.

15. After everyone speaks, your child begins his denials.

The interventionist is expert at cracking through his denials, with facts about the disease, and with facts from his behavior that bely his denials.

80

16. After your child has had his say.

The interventionist tells the child that he must go with him to the center. His questions are answered and his objections are fielded quite expertly. His bag is packed. His job has been notified, as has his school; he will not be fired or miss time, as the adolescent center has a school. His boss and his teacher may even be right there with you. At this point, his favorite uncle may help cajole him into quieter acceptance. Or, the interventionist may mention that his college tuition loan papers will be signed when he finishes treatment. Or, when things have been worked out with the judge. *Whatever* increases 'clout' will be used.

17. After your child has gone with the interventionist to treatment.

It is important that you all who have worked together to accomplish this sum up what has happened: That you have learned much about the disease and that you have cracked through, mightily, the silence and isolation that keeps this disease going. Encourage each other to maintain an open line of communication to help each other continue to learn about and recover from this disease.

25 Questions to Ask Treatment Centers

When you call, ask to speak to the program director. Remember that you are the consumer and if you are not happy with the answers you are getting, you can interview other program directors at other treatment centers.

The first three items on this list are the most important. Choose the facility that answers most of your questions favorably and seems to best meet your needs.

1. Does the center view alcoholism and addiction as a primary disease, or as a result of "underlying mental health problems"? (If there is any hedging about treating alcoholism as a primary disease, then hang up and call another center.)

2. Is the center AA oriented? Does it take clients to AA meetings while they are in treatment? Does it also have AA meetings *at* the center?

3. Does the center stress to their clients that they must go to "90 meetings in 90 days" when they leave the center? Does it stress that they must attend AA at least five to seven times per week for at least a year after they leave the center?

4. Can you tour the center without being pressured to send your child there?

5. Does the center have a family group to help you explore, without pressure, the idea of intervention and without a timetable for when you should do it?

6. Do you have an adolescent treatment program?

7. Is this an in-patient or out-patient program?

8. How many weeks or months does treatment last?

9. How close is the center to your home?

10. What does "evaluation" consist of at the center?

11. What is the success rate? (If seventy-five percent of the clients stay the length of treatment, attend AA, and stay sober, then the center is doing a good job.)

12. Are most of the counselors themselves recovering alcoholics? Have they been working in the field of addictions for at least two to five years?

13. Is the *family* treatment staff mainly made up of experienced Al-Anon people?

14. Does the center arrange for intervention in the home, or do you need to bring your child to the center to be evaluated?

15. What is the center's family treatment program like? How often is it? Is it individual or group?

16. Can parents visit the center?

17. Does the center have a school or tutorial program? Does it have a recreational program?

18. Is the center connected to a halfway house, if your child should need it?

19. What is the ongoing supervision at the halfway house? What are its requirements for attendance at AA?

20. Do they have follow-up for kids who don't go to a halfway house? What does the after-care program consist of?

21. What is the cost for the overall treatment program? How much is usually covered by insurance? Does that cover family treatment? Does that cover after-care for the child?

22. If the center can send an interventionist to your home, is there an additional charge?

23. If they are far away, does the cost include the center picking up your child and family and transporting all of you to and from the treatment center?

24. If the child is also mentally ill or "dually diagnosed," see the special chapter on that issue for more questions to ask the center.

25. Ask the program director to send you their printed informational literature in the mail. And make sure you have the name of the person with whom you've been speaking.

Reflection/Action Guide

Write On:

1. If you find yourself unable, at this point, to carry through with an intervention, write out your feelings about how you see the process and outcome.

2. Write out any fear-thoughts you may have about seeing a counselor to *explore* the idea of doing an intervention with your child.

3. What are the *facts* that compelled you to read this book?

Suggested Activities:

1. Allow yourself to just think about the *idea* of touring a treatment center for your child.

2. Go to young people's AA meetings and ask the kids there to help you with your feelings, especially your fears that your child will stop loving you.

3. Attend Al-Anon.

SEVEN

TOUGH LOVE IS TOO TOUGH FOR MOST OF US: HOW PROFESSIONALS CAN HELP DO THE INTERVENTION FOR YOU

Most family members are too frightened to give the alcoholic an ultimatum stating, "Get sober or else!" without having gone through lots of time in Al-Anon or counseling. But there are a number of effective steps you can take which will put you in charge, without having to necessarily resort to ultimatums and drastic actions.

Parents have all kinds of untapped ways for utilizing their power and authority. Depending on the circumstances, you might say:

—"If you want to go to college, first you have to go into treatment. Otherwise you pay your own way."

—"You're restricted. You can't go out. You can't have the car. You get no allowance."

—"You complete alcoholism evaluation and treatment, and then you can go out, have the car and your allowance."

—"If you get into trouble with the police, I will not bail you out. Instead, I will suggest strongly to the juvenile authorities that you be sent for treatment for what is causing all this behavior."

If you want additional help from professionals to make your child go to treatment, probation officers and schools as well as intervention specialists can help.

The juvenile justice system can do the intervention

Since many kids have gotten into legal trouble because of addiction, talking with the probation officer is probably the simplest and most immediate way for parents to arrange for their child to be confronted about his or her drug or alcohol problem.

No way is easy. However, once you learn methods for finding your way around the labyrinth of the juvenile justice system, you may find it much easier to rely on their assistance to do most of the confronting. And most likely, they will be very happy that you want them to help your child. Juvenile-justice professionals, who must often deal with hostile parents and children, as well as punitive facilities that are severely overcrowded, would often be grateful if all parents of addicted children would use them to help get kids to proper evaluation and treatment.

Many parents have a history of rescuing their children from the consequences of their disease. However, the vast majority of these parents are not thinking in such terms when they do the rescuing. They are merely acting instinctively as *any* parent would. Parents protect their child in order to protect their family's reputation as well as to protect the child from what they perceive as the only alternative: horrific jails or juvenile detention centers where kids are beaten or violated.

It never occurs to many parents that there is an alternative. Parents don't see that they can use the juvenile justice system as an *ally* to get their children to safety, to treatment. When a parent tells me, "Well, it's happened. He got arrested," I ask, "Have you talked to his probation officer?" Most of them have not.

I have often advised parents to call the probation officer and tell him or her the truth about alcohol and other drug use at home. Most probation officers are totally aware of what is going on with kids and alcohol and drugs.

If you've lost the name of the officer, or were never notified directly, you can phone the Family Court in your jurisdiction and get the person's name. Be sure you have been connected with the juvenile probation office and not the adult office.

Once you've established a truthful relationship with the officer, he is almost certain to help you help your child. When your son or daughter has to go back in front of a judge, the probation officer can put a forced choice to the adolescent: "Go to this program for treatment or go to detention." Needless to say, almost all the kids choose treatment.

A counselor told me of a mother she worked with whose son was her "prized possession." The son refused to come in for counseling sessions. So the counselor set up a meeting at a treatment facility with the mother and the son's probation officer. The mother felt it was humiliating to tell the officer that her son had a drug problem. But the probation officer just looked at her and asked, "Well, what do you want from me?"

"*Make* him go to treatment. But make it come from *you*, and leave me out of it," she answered.

The next time the officer saw her son he said, "You *have* to go to the meetings." He went to AA for the three years of probation. After the first nine months or so, he started to lose his resentment, and the meetings took. He's been sober for five years now.

School-based programs can do interventions

Another very effective way for parents to initiate intervention by an outsider is through organizations like IMPACT which develop school-based programs for prevention, education, and intervention.

In order to find out more about such programs, I spoke with Dr. Jeri Schweigler, director of National Training Associates, the organization that trains participants involved in the IMPACT League of Schools. Here's how they operate:

IMPACT currently has fifteen trainers who are experts in addictions. A number of former principals and teachers are among them.

Several of the trainers go to a participating school for one week. They link-up the school with a nearby addiction-treatment facility and they train and educate a core team of teachers and other school personnel to be able to identify addiction in students and to document their findings. Participation in the original core-team is strictly voluntary. There is *no* coercion to require school staff members who are hesitant to deal with the problem to become involved.

The core-team then gets referrals from other teachers and guidance counselors about students who may have a problem with alcohol or drugs. The team gathers documentation of each student's delinquent and truant behavior from teachers and counselors. Then the child is required to be assessed and diagnosed by professionals at the designated treatment facility.

If the child is found to be addicted, in consultation with the parents, he or she is sent to inpatient or outpatient treatment or directly to Alcoholics Anonymous or Narcotics Anonymous.

The beauty of the IMPACT process, and others like it, is that it works well for all concerned:

- Parents do not have to be "the heavies"; they can allow the schools to do the interventions, just as Employee Assistance Programs in industry have been doing so successfully for years with troubled adult employees.
- Frightened teachers do not have to stick their necks out; only the teachers who are actually *willing* to confront students form the original core-team.
- The cost to the school is reasonable. The contract with the cooperating treatment center stipulates that they make *no* charge for assessing and diagnosing referred students. Of course, for those who do go to treatment at the center, the cost of treatment is almost always 100% paid by the parents' third-party insurance.

Groups like IMPACT do much more than prepare schools for once-a-year interventions. They teach the core-team to educate the school, students, parents, and community, to understand addictions. And they help the core-team to grow and expand.

To inquire about getting IMPACT to come to your school or community, call or write:

National Training Association
P.O. Box 1476
Ukiah, CA 95482
Phone: (707) 468-0140

An intervention specialist can facilitate an intervention

Sometimes, when all else fails, it is necessary to force the child's hand and not allow him back into the house unless he goes to treatment.

90

However, it can't be said enough that it is so much easier to carry through if, (1) the parent gets much help from Al-Anon and counseling, and (2) the parent and intervention specialist use some of the techniques illustrated in the following story. The techniques are designed to "pave the road" to treatment so the child has almost no other choice, and to "close the door" on his street life.

In the following story, the son is seventeen. He has a stepfather that he does not like.* No matter how hard the stepfather has tried, the boy always has turned his back on him. He would not obey any of the rules of the house. He refused to come in at night at all, often staying out for days at a time. He kept visiting his real father who was more lenient since he felt very guilty for "not being there."

But it was the real father who called the counselor. He too was being used, and he saw that his son was going to die if no one did anything. He also knew that he was the one with the most clout; if anyone could get his son to listen, he could.

The father also was scared to death that he would lose whatever love his son had for him. Still, he couldn't ignore the facts. He couldn't lie to himself anymore.

When the intervention session was set up, they all agreed that the father should go to the son's home and participate with the mother and the stepfather. And all agreed that the choice should be put to the child: Go to treatment or go with your druggy friends. (The father had seen his son hanging out with a young man who lived down the street who was almost five years older than he was.)

Before the intervention began, the mother said, "He'll never agree to go to treatment."

The counselor said prophetic words: "If you let him go out of the home, and don't pay for anything, eventually he'll go to treatment because his friends will only cover for him financially for a weekend or so. Also, the older friend may very well tell your son that, as his parents, you cannot kick him out because legally he is not an adult and you have

---

*I chose to describe a step-parenting home to describe the methods that were used because so many parents feel that, with *two* homes involved, it is too difficult to attempt intervention.

91

to take care of him financially until he is. He may be encouraged to go to the police to try and force them to make you feed and clothe him."

In fact, the older friend *did* tell the son, "Your parents can't do that! They *have* to take care of you, no matter what!" And the son did "report" the parents. But the parents had taken some precautionary steps ahead of time by contacting the police and child protective services, so *that* door was blocked. And just as the counselor predicted, rather quickly his "friends" got tired of keeping him.

During the intervention at home, the son had come in and sat next to his real father. The counselor said who she was, where she worked, what she did, and that the whole family was concerned about his drug and alcohol behavior. She told him that they would like to tell him a few things about what had been going on. She said she wanted him to listen and he could talk later.

He rudely interrupted. Again, the counselor told him that he had to keep quiet, and that he'd have a chance to talk later.

It is most important that the counselor not allow the child to speak during the intervention until it is all over. There is a reason for this. The alcoholic child can "throw the parents off the track" and distract them with guilt and anger and disorient them in order to *avoid the real issue* of their drinking or drugging. The counselor cares very much for the child but also is very protective toward the parents in an intervention setting.

Keep in mind this slogan: "Let go and let the interventionist." It does not have to be as frightening for the parents as you might think. The ball will be in the *professional's* court. An intervention specialist has "seen it all" and knows what to expect and exactly how to handle it.

The family members all told how the drug behavior was affecting them. The counselor then told the son he would have to go to treatment. He said he wouldn't go and that he was leaving home.

The counselor said to the son, "You're leaving now, and I just want you to know that your parents will not let you back into the home unless you go to treatment." When he started to go to his bedroom to collect his possessions, she said to him, "No! Your parents are not allowing you to take all your things to sell them for drugs. You can go with your jacket, sweater, scarf, and hat because it is cold out there tonight." He was not allowed to go back into his bedroom.

He left. His parents were crying. His mother cried, "He'll never agree." The counselor reassured her, "Yes, he will. Make sure you have my number. Call the police now, and tell them what we talked about, about how the older friend will tell your son that you have to take him back in. Tell the police how we had this intervention. Tell them my name and phone number and which treatment center I work for."

The police found the son and questioned him. Of course, he denied any contact with drugs or alcohol. The parents urged the police to call Protective Services. They did so and Protective Services worked with the treatment agency in offering a room in a treatment facility for the child. The police told the son that there was alternative housing he could use if he needed it, at which point the boy refused and was driven back to his "friend's" place.

Later, the son called and wanted to come home. His friend had urged him to go home and just not stop the drugs. His parents said no.

Soon the other kids were tired of the situation with the police coming around. They were scared and urged him to try the "alternative housing." They were too stoned to realize it was a set-up for a drug treatment center.

Frustrated, he called his parents again and once more asked to come home. The parents told him that he could, just long enough to wait for the driver to pick him up and take him to the "alternative housing."

He was "blocked in" and had no alternative but the treatment center.

Reflection/Action Guide

Write on:

1. Describe your feelings about enlisting the aid of your child's probation officer or school to help him or her be made to go to treatment.

2. Describe how you (at least intellectually, if not emotionally) see your child not only "forgiving" you, but being grateful to you, when he has completed treatment, and he is functioning well, and his head is not fogged over.

3. Sometimes we think we've tried *everything* when all we've really tried is the *same* thing over and over. Often we're upset and can't see the whole picture until we write it down. Make a list of the strategies you may have used to get your child to treatment. Go through the chapter again and write out the things you have *not* yet tried.

Suggested Activities:

1. During this time, get help from a counselor who will be gentle with you. Shop around for the *right* counselor who will allow you to back off at the times when you are especially afraid.

2. Remember that there are now over 3 million recovering, sober alcoholics in Alcoholics Anonymous (and most of their families once felt like you do).

EIGHT

DURING TREATMENT AND AFTER: THE RECOVERY PROCESS CONTINUES

Treatment facilities vary, but there are some basic similarities in their programs and activities which can be highlighted.

In outpatient centers, a client will probably experience group therapy, individual therapy, see films on alcoholism, hear lectures on the disease of alcoholism, and receive a generally very good grounding in alcoholism education. In addition, in outpatient therapy, your child will still be experiencing the "outside world" on a regular basis, concurrently with the treatment. This can be valuable as the recovering adolescent can "reality test" everyday experiences several times a week, in individual and group therapy.

What does the child do in treatment?

For children who need a more structured environment for a while, the inpatient experience usually includes what the outpatient does, plus it often has these other features:

- A van transports the kids to a nearby AA or NA meeting several times a week. A counselor sits with them during the meetings, making sure they don't leave and making sure they pay attention.
- School or tutorial programs help them to keep up with school so

they don't fall behind.

- In adolescent centers, recreational therapy usually is scheduled daily.
- In between therapy sessions, even during free time, the kids usually are talking about "the program"—how they see, interpret and put to use, the concepts of AA.

"What do parents do while their children are in treatment?"

Meanwhile, at the same time a child is getting treatment, the parents also are continuing their own recovery from this family disease.

Jack and Vanna called me from Chicago asking me about their fourteen-year-old son, Tom, who was going to go to treatment in three days. "What do *we* do while he's gone?"

They were full of fear and excitement. Happy that their son, who had been giving them grief for three years, was finally, tearfully, going to get help, they wanted to make sure that they provided the kind of homelife when he came home that would ensure his happiness forever.

I developed this task list for them.

- Start having fun. When was the last time you went to dinner and a movie without worrying about whether the house would burn down by the time you got home? (Their son always passed out while smoking.)
- Go to Al-Anon. Go to family treatment.
- Get the other children to Alateen meetings so they can begin to recover too.
- Start *believing* that you did not cause this disease.
- Talk to each other about your irrational guilt, and all the "tiny" ways it manifests itself, insidiously, in your conversation.
- Use your family and Al-Anon treatment to reinforce the understanding that even though you made regular mistakes (which *every* parent does) you still have the right, *and the duty*, to enforce rules; that you do *not* have to "make up" for the past; that you can't "walk on eggs" when your child comes home! It certainly won't make a bit of difference in his recovery process, but it will drive you bananas to try to live up to your expectations of yourselves!

98

Is a halfway house the answer?

Many very good adolescent treatment centers send most kids to halfway houses after the inpatient experience is ended. Here are some questions for parents to consider when making the decision, with the center, about what might be best for *your* child:

- Is your guilt so overwhelming that you will find it difficult to say no to anything after your child arrives home?

- Are you so anxious about the possibility of a relapse that you feel overwhelmed when you think about dealing with your child during his early sobriety? (Parents *cannot* cause a relapse; this is no more possible than it was for you to cause your child to contract the disease in the first place.)

- If your child winds up not following the necessary house rules (and those that ensure his sobriety), are you emotionally able to *then* make sure he goes to a halfway house? Or would it be easier to place him there from the beginning?

- Do you have the time to give your child the structure he will need? If you are a single parent who works outside the home, I have found that the answer is usually no even for "supermoms."

It is terribly important that you explore these questions as dispassionately as possible. *Most* parents cannot provide this amount of structure. And no rational decision can be made by superimposing guilt on top of an understandable fear about providing the kind of after-care that a halfway house can.

Many children and adolescents need 24-hour-a-day supervision after they leave treatment. Most need to be chauffeured to AA or NA meetings once or twice a day. Most need to regularly confer with counselors and recovering peers about their anxieties and mood swings which are a normal, but difficult, part of early recovery.

Most parents work. Most parents and children need *time* to recover or just establish good communications with each other (this is where good therapy is so important).

Most parents and kids need these extra months to be separate and recover without the added anxiety-provoking intimacy that living together would invite.

One family's decision—and healing

Nadine and Ralph are the parents of Tom and Jonathan, their teenage sons. Tom is Nadine's son from a former marriage and Jonathan is Ralph's son from his previous marriage. Nadine and Ralph are both non-alcoholic, oldest children of alcoholic homes. They've been married to each other for five years. Their adjustment to each other has been complicated by a number of alcoholism issues.

When they were first married, their sons' unusually intense resentments toward their parents seemed odd. Fairly recently, Nadine and Ralph discovered that both sons had developed alcohol and drug habits, thus explaining much of the irrational hostility.

The whole family went to see a therapist, but the therapist blamed the childrens' alcoholism on the new marriage and didn't focus on the drinking and drugging. She believed that it would "all work out" once the family communications were clearer.

Fortunately, Nadine and Ralph were certain their sons had to stop drinking and drugging and managed to get them both to treatment. But unfortunately, they both brought a *tremendous* sense of guilt and responsibility with them into the marriage; felt responsible for anything that went wrong and felt angry that the children "rained on their parades." They had worked very hard to make everything all right again and to get where they wanted to be.

Given this set of circumstances, when Ralph and Nadine came to me for counseling, I suggested that they allow the children to enter halfway houses for about six months after treatment. The boys wanted that too. I suggested that the kids would have a chance to work past their early sobriety mood-swings before they came home. They could also get some sobriety under their belts while they looked anew at their relationship with their parents. Examining the remarriage at a sober distance, with a good therapist, took a lot of the venom out of the feelings of both boys.

And Ralph and Nadine needed some time alone together in their new marriage. They both entered an ACOA group (for adult children of alcoholics). They found the group through their children's treatment center and began the work of letting go of the life-long habit of taking on the responsibility for everyone else's feelings.

Nadine and Ralph also learned that much of their anger was around issues in life that were just not all that important. They began to see their tense lifestyles, to see how they had viewed any crack in it as terrible.

So much healing needed to be separately accomplished that Nadine and Ralph started to relish the time apart from their children—especially when they began to perceive their *own* growth.

Instead of lamenting over newly-discovered unhealed areas of life, it is much more sensible and effective to just admit to this fact and get on with using the valuable time apart. With Nadine and Ralph and the kids all in treatment, years of therapy were accomplished in a much shorter time. The healing I've seen in countless other families who all go to treatment after sobriety is amazing.

When making the choice of whether or not to send your son or daughter to a halfway house or whether to bring your child directly home from the treatment center, remember that this is a choice and that the answer is not fixed for all time. All of us forget that most of life's decisions are not irrevocable.

Also, don't try to guiltily turn your home into a halfway house and once again center all the family's energy on the alcoholism disease. The opposite approach is what will get your family well much sooner.

Learning disabilities: A danger of relapse

Most alcoholism treatment facilities give patients written materials when they leave, that instruct them on how not to "build up to a drink." Danger signals are presented and discussed. Strategies and inspiration for staying sober are provided.

For teens and pre-teens, the problem issues and danger signals often are different from those of adults. One such issue is the matter of learning disabilities.

What does that mean? Usually, to fit the definition of "learning disabled," a child *must* have at least a normal I.Q. It is definitely not the same as "retarded." Just the opposite. Many learning-disabled children are quite bright but exhibit problems in spelling, reading, writing, or comprehension. Ask them to write something, and they put the letters down backwards. Or they can't spell correctly even though they can get great grades in other areas.

There are training programs that can do a lot for learning-disabled children. Many schools understand the problems and can help correct them once a child has been tested and identified.

If a child with a learning disability goes back to school and starts doing poorly again, no matter how hard he tries, it's going to be hard, in the midst of that failure, to fight off the desire to drink. That is the greatest danger in not dealing with the problem immediately.

Reflection/Action Guide

Write On:

1. Write out all the ways you anticipate finding it difficult to say no to your child about *anything*, when he or she is newly sober.

2. Write out all your irrational beliefs about thinking you could "prevent a relapse" and why you imagine you will have to "walk on eggs" when your child leaves treatment.

3. If you are panicking at the thought of learning disabilities, write out how you may have the tendency to panic (as many alcoholic family members do) at *any* new situation you encounter and how the situation often is resolved with much less struggle than you had anticipated.

Suggested Activities:

1. Discuss what you wrote in questions one and two of the "Write On" questions with your counselor.

2. If you are touring a treatment facility, tour the halfway house connected with the center, too. It is better to get rid of nagging fears about all the facilities from the start.

3. Discuss with a counselor, very realistically, whether you are too emotionally drained from the alcoholic's devastation to deal with a newly sober child and all the extreme mood swings that are typically manifested. Begin to explore your feelings about the possibility of sending your child, after treatment, to a halfway house. Examine both the pro's and the con's.

NINE

IF YOUR CHILD ALSO IS MENTALLY ILL

For the child who is addicted to alcohol or other drugs and also is mentally ill, finding the right treatment is especially important. Some parents find a treatment center with a staff that understands exactly what to do with an addicted child, but is baffled by what to do with the mentally ill child. Others find centers with people who *think* they know what to do, but do not have the necessary expertise in the mental health area. Still other parents may take their child to a therapist who understnads mental illness and how to treat it, but if the child continues to take alcohol or drugs, the getting well process will be thwarted. Too many times, the drinking and drugging is seen as a byproduct of the mental illness, and not as a separate illness that needs its own treatment.

Elaine, a mother I met while I was on a speaking tour in New England, solved this problem for her daughter, but only after several years of anguish.

Elaine's story: My daughter also is schizophrenic

Having always seen myself as a wife and mother, my greatest fear while the kids were growing up was to fail as a parent. That fear was realized when I found out my daughter, Bertha, was binge-drinking at the age of fourteen. And then, when she was sixteen, she started to have frequent hallucinations. At first I thought it was because of the drinking, but both problems turned out to be chronic. Eventually she was diagnosed as being schizophrenic.

I took her to several mental health centers in the first few years. She would get better and then would be released. But she wouldn't keep taking the medication, so she'd wind up needing to be taken to another hospital. Each time, they recognized the schizophrenia, but no one diagnosed the alcoholism.

Generally, my encounters with helping professionals weren't good. I always believed the counselor knew so much. And the prevailing philosophy at the time was that schizophrenia was caused by the mother. Things have changed quite a lot. But then, that was the message that was strongly implied to me, her mother.

I was afraid to answer *any* questions about Bertha. It seemed like no matter what I said, it was interpreted as some deep-seated problem that *I* hadn't taken care of.

At the same time, I was trying to deal with my alcoholic husband. So I was so afraid of everything. At certain times, I even felt jealous around Bertha. She was the favorite in the household. My husband *used* her against me; he used everyone to make me jealous. Even strangers. It was just particularly hard when he used our daughter. And then I felt so ashamed that I could feel jealousy toward my own child.

I was always told, in therapy, that it was my fault. I was told it was my fault that I had stayed with my husband. If I hadn't, so the thinking went, then maybe my daughter would not have gotten so sick. These were not specialists in alcoholism. All they saw was the schizophrenia. At the time very, very few places recognized that there could be alcoholism *and* illness in the same person.

While Bertha was in the hospital, I was trying to deal with my husband, too. We were separated at that point and I was trying to get him to go to treatment. At the same time, I was trying to help Bertha plan her weekends at home. It was a lot to try to do. I was desperate.

The counselor and I were getting very hostile with each other. Bertha was twenty and in her sixth psychiatric center. In all this time, she hadn't gotten any better. She was even sneak-drinking at the hospital, and her alcoholism was still not being addressed. When we would talk about Bertha, I would say, "But she's an alcoholic too, not

106

just schizophrenic." The therapist wanted me to accept that Bertha had a mental illness only. She would say to me, "You know an awful lot about alcoholism, but you don't know anything about mental illness."

They brought in the psychiatrist. He was very annoyed with me. He saw me as arrogant because I knew a lot more about alcoholism than they did. I felt despairing, because I felt they *should* have known more about alcoholism than they did! *They* were the professionals! Why did I know more then they did, or more than they were willing to find out?

When I first brought Bertha to their treatment facility, I told the psychiatrist and social worker who met with me that Bertha came from an alcoholic home and had abused alcohol and other drugs. They asked me what I had done about it, so I explained that I went to Al-Anon and that I had learned to detach. As soon as I used that word, they jumped on me. Because Bertha was herself detached, in a *schizophrenic* way, they inferred that my Al-Anon type detachment got her that way. As if Al-Anon's sense of the word "detachment" was a cause of schizophrenic detachment! They didn't even bother to ask me what I meant by the word. And I was too scared, too unable to explain it. All I could feel was guilt and fear and confusion. They just went on with their questions and diagnosing and I felt powerless to stop them. I even forgot that I objected to their changing the meaning of detachment on me. After that initial intake, all the sessions were predicated on the basis that Bertha was sick because I was.

When I told the psychiatrist that I loved my husband, he said I was crazy. I told him that, right or wrong, that was how I felt. I said to him "How do you feel about mentally ill people? You still love them, don't you, even if they do things that you don't like?" He didn't have a straight answer for that.

Later, I found out that his son had committed suicide. I wondered if he had been on drugs or alcohol, and also if the doctor was in his *own* family-denial about alcoholism.

When Bertha jumped off the low roof of the hospital and broke her ankle trying to get away to find a bar, I asked the "experts" at the center if they *now* believed that she had a drinking problem? (This was not the first time she had gotten into serious trouble over alcohol—dangerous situations, all of them.) I got very angry with them and said, "Would you have believed she had a problem with alcohol if she had jumped from a third-floor window and died? Or would you say she just

tal illness and committed suicide?" They didn't answer me.
I confronted them about their ignoring her alcoholism, they
red me. I didn't know how to confront them about their
They were the professionals. I felt with them like I was
constantly defending myself.

For example, I continued going to Al-Anon, but then the therapist
implied there was something wrong with me, because I continued
going after I was separated from my husband. However, I also was
blamed for having stayed with my husband in the first place, with the
implication that this made Bertha sicker. So I was going away from
those "family sessions" feeling worse each time.

My Al-Anon meetings were telling me that I did the best I could. And I
wanted to believe that—because I *did* do the best I could, at the time. I
upped the number of meetings I went to; I had to, because I would
leave "family therapy" feeling so rotten. We were all so angry with each
other; we weren't getting anywhere. They blamed me for causing her
schizophrenia; I blamed them for not addressing her alcoholism; I
knew that if they did, she could get at least partially well. But Bertha
stayed sick. So when I clearly saw that nothing was getting anywhere, I
dropped out of the family sessions.

After searching for two more years, I found an alcoholism treatment
center that also knew what to do with schizophrenic alcoholics.
Bertha's now off the alcohol and attending AA and taking her
medication on a daily basis. She's much better.

Expert advice: What to do, where to go?

Many alcoholics display symptoms of severe psychotic disorders
while drinking or drugging, or during withdrawals, but they are not
true psychotics. Such alcoholics suffer from alcohol or other drug-
induced mental illness.

How does one know if a child is truly mentally ill, or if the symptoms
will go away, once the alcohol and other drugs are out of their systems?
Dr. Jerry Shulman and I talked about this, and other vital aspects of
treatment.

Recognizing the "dually diagnosed"

"More and more referrals to chemical-dependence treatment specialists are coming from psychiatrists and mental health practitioners,"

Dr. Shulman explained. "You know, I remember *never* getting referrals from psychiatrists. In fact, because they're psychiatrists, they are more apt to have a caseload that includes more psychotic people who also are alcoholic. But what many misinformed alcoholism counselors are doing to these people who are what I call 'dually diagnosed' is they are denying them an opportunity to get well. What the counselor often says is, 'This guy really is strange. He's not alcoholic; there's something else wrong with him. We've got to send him to the local mental-health center.' So they send him there, he gets put on medication, and he gets to be okay. The people at the mental-health center are pleased and say to him, 'Why don't you go outside at night? You can get a pass.' So he goes outside and gets drunk. This poor guy bounces back and forth. And there's no reason for that to happen. There's absolutely no reason.

"What *do* you do? You stabilize him on the medication. You treat him for chemical dependence. You let the client know he is dually diagnosed, that he has both problems. People who are mentally ill have to do the same thing for their chemical dependence as other alcoholics and addicts, in order to maintain their sanity."

Is it temporary toxic psychosis?

"We have a psychiatrist on our staff who can evaluate who is psychotic and who is not," Dr. Shulman explained.

"Is it true," I asked him, "that you should wait six months after sobriety to know whether it's a real psychosis?"

Dr. Shulman answered, "That would be wonderful if you had the time! Often, we must make a quicker diagnosis. If the psychosis is from alcohol or other drugs, it will be manifest only during active drinking or withdrawal. If it is manifest in someone who's no longer in withdrawal, then it's not toxic, or chemically-induced psychosis.

"We can monitor this because we know that psychotic-type reactions to the chemicals in alcohol and drugs happen within a certain time frame. But we'll also want to know who else in that person's family has a depression, for instance. I'm talking about people who have a clearly defined depressive disorder because these run in families. Just knowing that depression runs in that family makes it more likely this may be a real depression. I'll want to know about the depression during periods when there's been *no* drinking or drug taking.

"I'm saying that you do have to get the person off the chemicals, but you don't necessarily have to wait six months before you can do a good evaluation. There are paper-and-pencil tests; psychological tests. There also are blood tests for some kinds of depression. There are many different things one can do to make an evaluation."

Finding a treatment center

"How do you find a place that treats both disorders?" I asked Dr. Shulman.

"I suggest a parent calls up and immediately says to the people at the treatment center, 'My child is chemically dependent and also is acting out in very bizarre ways that I think might mean she also has a severe mental problem. I want to know whether you're willing to evaluate and treat this child.'

"Parents should ask a number of questions, including: What are you going to do for my child? Who's going to adjust his or her medication, if it is needed? Do you have a psychiatrist? How frequently will my child have an opportunity to be seen by the psychiatrist? Will he or she be tested?

"The answers should be: The psychiatrist will see your child on admission. The psychiatrist will be available to prescribe or adjust any needed medication. An evaluation will be done. The treatment center *will* work with the psychiatrist.

"A lot of times the psychiatrist needs to be available only a few times during the whole treatment. Other times, they need to be there every other day. It depends on what's needed. A psychiatrist should be able to be on call.

"Now, if the treatment center responds over the phone, without having observed the child, 'No, we can't take kids like that; he's probably just chemically dependent,' then I wouldn't send anybody to them because that speaks of a clinical irresponsibility."

If you feel weary that there is so much to cope with, remember that the extra effort it may require to find a competent facility for the treatment of both disorders will *greatly* lessen your worry in the future. Fortunately, many alcoholism centers now recognize and successfully treat dually-diagnosed adults and young people. To find the one closest to you, start by calling the numbers on the hotline page and interview them on the phone using the questions Dr. Shulman

110

suggests.

Many persons in AA have several disorders, and are sober, and sane, for many, many years. They and their families despaired as you do, never thinking they'd make it. But they have.

Reflection/Action Guide

Write On:

1. Describe your child's behavior history, as you have seen and know it, (a) before the drinking or drugging ever started, (b) during it, and (c) after episodes of using. This could be quite beneficial for the evaluator.

2. Describe your very natural feelings of anger towards your child and your guilt about the anger.

3. Describe the feelings of shame you have. (They, too, are very normal feelings.)

Suggested Activities:

1. When you begin to feel overwhelmed, remind yourself that treatment is getting much more sophisticated and *can* help your child.

2. Call centers on the hotline page and explore their brochures; talk to them about their treatment plans for dually-diagnosed children.

SECTION THREE
CRAZYMAKING ISSUES

TEN

CAUGHT IN THE MIDDLE: WHEN ADULT CHILDREN OF ALCOHOLICS ARE ALSO PARENTS OF ALCOHOLICS

What's happened since you've grown up?

For most children of alcoholics, when you become adults, even though you may not drink, you still are affected by the disease. While you think you are okay, your behavior indicates you're not.

Some of you didn't drink. Some of you teetotalled and assumed that would fix it—forever. Some of you "got into" religion. Some of you "got into" sex. Some "got into" work; others "got into" gambling. Perhaps you "got into" eating disorders.

Whatever the case, you were never able to lay to rest the anxieties about your childhood. You *thought* you did because you were busy, because you achieved.

Either you were very, very rigid, or very, very lackadaisical. You put yourself and others down, if you were rigid, for not towing the line at all times and under all conditions. It was not uncommon for you not to take a day's sick leave in thirteen years. You became ill because of this, but were secretly proud of it. (Or, maybe not so secretly.)

You beat yourself about your disorganization, if you were lackadaisical. But, you compensated by calling yourself "flexible," and "adaptable." You knew no middle ground. You scorned it, actually.

117

You didn't see the forest for the trees, even though you were dying to "see" something that made sense. You felt "weird" much of the time, but you didn't know where to put that weirdness or what to attribute it to. You love the exception; you are bored with the rule.

On the surface, all seems okay. But often, all the activity and success cannot end the uneasiness lurking beneath the surface.

The denials, the diversions

One corporate head, interviewed in a magazine, said *nothing* stopped him from succeeding. Many power-drivers in business are alcoholics or adult children of alcoholics, and success becomes an acceptable way to channel the anxiety, to get applause that makes one feel like they are okay, that one's parents may finally be pleased. Everybody—society, the world, etc.—comes to symbolize the parents. "Tell me I'm wonderful. Then, maybe, *I'll* believe it." But ACOA's don't need just to *divert* from the anxiety and the restlessness; they need to deny its very cause—the alcoholism.

The adult child of alcoholics who also is the parent of alcoholics learned the alcoholic-denial-behavior that said, "My dad still has a job, so he can't be an alcoholic. *I* still have a good job. I'm sending myself through secretarial school at night. I have a late-model car. I'm *not* a dysfunctional adult child of an alcoholic.

"My child gets A's in school, so I feel okay. I don't have to look at the fact that he is 'four sheets to the wind.' "

Other denials ACOA's commonly use are, "You can't be an alcoholic:

- If you have a job.
- If you never lost a job.
- If you get promotions.
- If you are talented.
- If your home looks elegant.
- If you look polished and speak well.
- If you read lots of books.
- If you jog.

- If you take vitamins.
- If you are nutrition-conscious.
- If your kids are bright.
- If your husband is successful. (Would he be there with you if you were an alcoholic? Of course not! So you aren't one!)"

For example, a mother tells me about her son saying, "But, he's still doing well. There are so many areas of his life where he is doing well. He is basically such a kind person. He is so generous with others. He has such a sense of family. He's a wonderful teacher. He doesn't make a lot of money, but his values are good. He doesn't place emphasis on making money or on materialism; he's much more interested in being a decent human being. In his music, he's *so* involved—so *passionate* about his art!"

Her description of her son is her way of saying he does not have the disease of alcoholism. Denial, diversion, perfectionism, and anger are all behaviors which describe adult children of alcoholics who also are parents of alcoholics.

Getting help for the anger

Sandra's eighteen-year-old, Rob, made her "see red" even if he just walked into a room where she was. Her hostility toward him, and his toward her, started long before his active drinking. For Sandra it was so intense that it actually hurt.

"It's this big *glob!*" she cried. "I don't know where to start dealing with it. It's never going to get taken care of. It's too big."

Sandra was tiny, with red hair and a lovely face. Her petite elegance belied her way of life. Hers was a coarse household: it reminded me of exactly how I grew up.

Most of those in the group Sandra was in were ACOA's. That's not why they joined the group, ostensibly. They came in "for problems." They talked mostly, at first, about their spouses who were drinking away all the money. Then, guiltily, they spoke of their children, who were "so much like their fathers." They seemed surprised that nearly everyone in their group had kids "like that."

What was even more shocking to them was the discovery that 90 percent of them, whose children were addicted, also were themselves children of alcoholics.

"Did I make him like that?" was the recurring question we had to deal with. When we thought the issue had been settled with one of the group members, the guilt would pop up again in another member. While it was somewhat comforting to see that the script was the same (that there was a positive "cookie-cutter" effect going on), the guilt also seemed infectious.

When the guilt calmed, the anger and the depression began to surface. And that was what seemed too 'globby' to deal with. It was one big glob of feeling. *Of course* it was too much to handle. It needed to be sorted out—cut down into manageable bites.

In Sandra's case, it was all entangled: the anger, fear, and frustration toward the alcoholic parent—and the same intense feelings towards her child. Plus the guilt from knowing she was "pouring the past" onto Rob, her son. More stuff to sort out, to lay aside, kept creeping back into the glob, threatening to make it too much to handle again.

Sandra was one of the lucky ones in the group: she already *knew* she was angry with her addicted parent. The others weren't actually denying, in the sense of 'lying,' when they said they weren't angry. They were totally unaware of any feelings of anger.

Those same persons realized that it would take awareness of feelings before they could hope to lay the past to rest. To allay their fears of hopelessness about *ever* getting in touch with those feelings, I told them about myself.

I've found that it often takes *years* of listening, patience, hope, to let the sharing of others in groups filter in through my petrified layers of fear.

I had been involved for many, many years with families of alcoholics. My own mother had been very ill with addiction and hatred. She used to joke about my having been an accident.

One day, on a train going to my home in Maryland, from Massachusetts, I was thinking rather peacefully about the scenery, and all of a sudden, the realization came to me that my mother had not loved me. I felt terribly sad, and silently cried all the way to Philadelphia. I couldn't stop crying. I felt strange, knowing that I wasn't feeling anger, but very, very intense *sadness.* I knew I was doing some letting go, and I was sad about that, too. Just a *lot* of sadness. When it was over, I felt older, in a good way.

I remember feeling surprised that I hadn't worked on this issue; in fact, I thought I had avoided it. But, I had gotten my body to the recovery groups, and even though I worked on other issues, the program was washing over me.

Instead of it being like surgery without anesthetic, the letting go process was so gentle and mindful of my fears, that it just *did* it to me. I didn't have to force it.

Experiences like this (my own and those of others)—*all* the time— tell me that treatment works. We all think we're beyond help in certain issues and that the craters of pain left over from childhood can *never* be healed. That's so untrue.

This isn't to say that we shouldn't "work" at all, in treatment, and "stretch ourselves" at times. But, instead, that when we are weary, and cannot grow one more inch by ourselves, God often does for us what we cannot do for ourselves, if we let Him.

Whittling down the anger

When Sandra confronts her anger, now, she sits down and asks herself, "Who am I mad at?" She assigns percentages to each: 10 percent is heavy annoyance at the people who keep knocking on the door when she's busy, looking for the people who used to live there; 3 percent is directed toward the local grocer who never seems to have change, especially when she's in a hurry; 25 percent is at her father who was slow (Was it always on purpose? His sly smile when it happened seemed to indicate to her that this was probably so.); 42 percent is at her son, *everyday; and the other 20 percent is at herself for not being able to stop feeling angry!*

After sorting it out in this way, it was so much easier for her to tone it all down, and actually get rid of some of that anger baggage. When the anger at the grocer was seen in perspective, she was pretty much able to tell herself: "The heck with it!"

This ability stems from her knowledge of the Serenity Prayer:
"God, grant me the serenity
   To accept the things I cannot change.
The courage to change the things I can.
   And the wisdom to know the difference."
As for the collectors who kept knocking on the door not believing

the former tenants had really moved, she promised herself to be able to look to see who was coming, and not have to *again* explain that they had moved. And she promised herself that she did not have to feel guilty. (She knew from experience that the guilt would "just go" if she did what she was supposed to do for a long enough time.)

Those responses took care of the anger toward the grocer and the collectors, but what about the rest?

As soon as she saw that the extra burden she was putting on herself for not being able to drop her anger was silly, she was able to whittle it down.

And the anger toward her son? She tried doing what AA suggested: every day, for three weeks, she asked God to give him health, wealth, and happiness—everything she would wish for herself.

Now, it didn't start out that way! Her first prayers were, "Go *get* him, God!" When she screamed that out, she eventually could laugh. She said to her Higher Power, "You *know* I don't like him! Tell you what, God. You make him well so he'll be nice. Okay?"

"I'm *not* going to pray for Him!"

And when she hurt real bad, she prayed, "God, help me. Help me to let go. Let me not fear his worst."

Some days she could not bring herself to pray for her son. That's okay. Other days, when she felt good, she forgot. Isn't it nice that she felt good enough to forget? It's good to remember to pray, but it's also good to feel good.

Letting others live—so that you can live

Thelma called me from Tulsa. Much of her anger centered around the fact that her alcoholic father had gotten sober, and after a ten-year absence, had returned home. Her mother welcomed him.

"How can he just *sit* there, watching television, being happy, after all the pain he caused? He should *pay* for it! Look at all *I* still have to put up with!" Thelma cried.

She was a divorced teacher and mother of a twelve-year-old who was starting to sneak-drink. She taught ballet in the evenings, and had accumulated an enviable coin collection. Everyone thought she "had it made"—especially her brothers who married young, worked hard, didn't finish high school, and each had children from former marriages to support.

122

Thelma had settled for teaching. She wanted to have the courage to try her hand at running her own ballet school full-time. She was good enough, but she didn't try. This was because she realized that if she failed, she would lose the dream. And the dream was more exciting than the reality. She felt so frustrated with herself.

And she wanted it all—now. Only thirty-eight, she thought she should be accomplished in four careers, own $10,000 worth of stereo equipment and be part owner in a vacation home. She didn't want to wait for anything and was annoyed when her mother reminded her that "when she was young, people didn't get things like that at all, or they were in their fifties when they achieved them."

Over-achievement. . . impatience to the point of depression and anxiety . . . perfectionism . . . low boiling point . . . inability to trust . . . inability to be pleased . . . this is a portrait of an adult child of an alcoholic.

Is Thelma *really* that angry at her father? Or, is it masking anger at her son that she can't admit without guilt? Or, is she *mostly afraid* that she'll *never* get what *she* wants, or even *know* what she wants?

It is so much easier to be gracious with other people when we are able to enjoy what we have, when we have hope that we can continue to do so. Even if those others are people in our families who have hurt us.

That personal joy in what we already have gained and accomplished gives us a blanket in which we can wrap ourselves that no past injury can penetrate.

We can't change the past. We can't change "him or her." We *can* enjoy who we are now—in the present, with help. "But they should *pay!*" we feel. We *all* have felt that, and still do, sometimes. But, we never stop beating our heads against a brick wall until we get sick and tired of being sick and tired. We *cannot* "let live" unless we are living, now.

Don't compare your progress in treatment with the progress of others

Adult children of alcoholics are always comparing their progress in treatment with the progress of others. If you had heart disease, you certainly wouldn't beat yourself for not getting well at the same rate as the person in the next hospital bed. You would be concerned; you would feel down about it; but you would not blame yourself.

This is another area where we must start to see alcoholism as a disease. It is not a matter of a weakness or a strength of character—this *getting* the disease; nor are those factors in the *treatment* of it. After all, if I had diarrhea, you certainly would not think of feeling morally superior to me and proclaiming, "Well, I don't know what's wrong with *you*! *My* bowel movements are firm!" It is just as absurd to feel that anyone is morally or intellecutally superior because they did not get alcoholism or because their treatment seems to be "taking" faster in them. Fortunate they are. Superior they are not.

This comparing one's progress to that of another in treatment also is a *manifestation* of the disease: alcoholism's constant attempt to drag us down, one way or another.

If we can't find any other thing to put ourselves down about, we compare ourselves to *anyone* who is "doing better."

When people call me for telephone counseling, invariably one out of every three calls is from a person who says, "Oh, you're going to think I'm so stupid, but . . . ."

They go on to tell me that they are separated from their alcoholic husbands, and they are still entangled and spinning; that they can't deal with his alcoholism *and* their son's alcoholism and drug addiction, and do all that the program of recovery they are in asks them to do.

I say to them, "What is the program actually asking you to do? Where is it expecting that you 'be at' now? Has anyone actually said that you should be ashamed of yourself because you are not more well and detaching so wonderfully from the whole mess? Is anyone actually saying that to you?"

"Oh, no," she answers. "It's just that *I* think I should be further along. I should be doing better and not feeling so bad; dealing with this whole thing better. After all, *I know* the answers. I *go* to the recovery meetings!"

She says she takes her husband back; she let's her child back in; she gives him his allowance even though he drinks; she signs the paper to let him back in college when she said she wouldn't; she pays her husband's car loan when he is seeing another woman; etc, etc. And she always says, afterwards, "Oh, I'm so stupid. How could I *do* such a thing? I *know* better! I've been in Al-Anon for a year-and-a-half! I go to counseling! I help others in the same mess. I'm so ashamed; I could never tell others that I did that. It's like I never got any help. *When* will I learn?!"

We absolutely forget that alcoholism (as AA says) is "cunning, baffling, and powerful." We mouth that phrase and it sounds good. But, do we take it in? Do we think about what cunning, baffling and powerful really mean?

The words mean that alcoholism gets us extremely and bizarrely embroiled emotionally with an alcoholic. It is so powerful that when we crawl to the disease—we think we are crawling to the alcoholic.

It makes us forget we are not dealing with the alcoholic; that what is coming out of his mouth is the disease. That his actions are those of his disease. That he is brain-soaked with alcohol.

Since it is absolutely necessary for you, at times, to take two or three steps backward before you can go on the next part of your journey in getting well, you must accept some backward steps, and not put yourself down. For, when you spend valuable time putting yourself down, you stay stuck in that part of the journey, and make less overall progress.

So how do you get unstuck? Keep it simple. When you find yourself saying, "I should have," or "I shouldn't have," tell yourself, "Stop it. The heck with it. Big deal. So what?"

And then change your thoughts, and go on and do something else that is pleasant—watch TV, read, go walking. Make yourself feel good about yourself.

Practice self-acceptance. In three weeks, if this can be your daily growth activity, you will find yourself far ahead of schedule—as far as where you want to be—in terms of being able to find peace of mind, make decisions, and carry through.

Reflection/Action Guide

Write On:

1. If you are an ACOA, did you "get into" work, sex, alcohol, gambling, eating?

2. What anger or fear did you think you "left behind" in childhood that has, in reality, chronically been a problem?

Suggested Activities:

Increase the "fluff" time in your life; i.e. films, books (not on therapy), concerts, laughter time. Nothing speeds up recovery like fun. Not introspection. Not "working on it." Nothing.

This "fluff" time must not be in pursuit of excellence. It must not be in activities that involve awards or rewards, winning, seeing levels of achievement, or any other kind of comparing or "proving." It must be simply for *fun*!

ELEVEN

ALCOHOLIC GAMES: WHEN YOUR ALCOHOLIC EX-SPOUSE ADDS TO YOUR TROUBLES

Single parents have more than enough traumatic issues to deal with. But, to be the separated spouse of an alcoholic—and have an addicted child or children—can seem much too much to bear. Yet sorting out the problems takes a *big* chunk out of the despair and relieves the panic.

What are some of the issues in this kind of situation?

- Your ex-spouse tries to woo your child away with gifts, while not even giving you your court-ordered child support.

- Your child sees your ex-spouse as "Santa," and you feel you must compete, but you don't have the money or the inclination to do so.

- Your child's disease makes him use you against your ex-spouse, and you are understandably very afraid to "threaten" your child with alcoholism treatment. He will "go live with his father." the child says.

- You start legal proceedings against your spouse (for visitation, custody, child support, alimony) and guilt and fear of losing a chance of reconciliation forever sets in, and you want to drop it all.

- Your ex-spouse got the court, somehow, to see him (or her) as the "rational" one (even though he or she is drinking alcoholically), and your "ex" was awarded custody or visitation rights, even though he is violent or sexually abusive. *And* all this is intensified by your older children drinking—and you don't know what to tackle first, second, or what.

These are the problems which I believe most commonly occur, and they are they ones which are the most urgent to deal with. They absolutely *can* be whittled down, substantially.

Dealing with the put-downs.

Sometimes, we discount our feelings by comparing them to "more traumatic" ones of other people. For instance, if you are not dealing with a violent ex-spouse, but "just" with an alcoholic "ex" who is trying to play you against your child, you say, "Well, I'm not dealing with violence, so, I *shouldn't* be so upset with 'just' this problem."

I believe that alcoholic family members discount their feelings to a much greater degree than other people do.

What is not looked at, in this self-degradation, is the chronic soul erosion that goes on in the process. When trying to raise your kids alone, and dealing with an alcoholic ex-spouse, it feels like a no-win situation. You *do* wonderfully. You take care of the daily parenting situations that other homes with two parents do much more easily: the chauffering, the comforting, the laundry, cooking, cleaning, shopping, helping with homework, tending to pets, ballet, scraped knees. At the same time, you take care of your child's fears that "Dad will never be seen again," with the turmoil that always occurs after a visit with the alcoholic parent, when it usually takes three days to get back to normal.

Even after you've done a terrific job with the kids, you always ask yourself, "What have I left undone? What emotional needs of the children have I not taken care of?" And of course there are some! You are human.

But, in additiion to putting yourself down for things not done, you talk with your separated spouse (whom you have mixed feelings about) and he puts you down for being "a saint," "perfect," and "doing too much"! You feel terrible, like you've again overstepped your parameters, and intruded into everyone else's life, not allowing them to live it on their own.

You believe you can't win—that it's never enough, what you do—and yet it's always too much.

Look at this logically: *Do* you do enough? If so, it'll be too much, according to your alcoholic ex-spouse. Suppose you do *not* do enough? You know you'll be remiss in what you must do for your child.

But, most important, remember that his criticism is based on lies. Al-Anon says that you can't please an alcoholic. I'd take that one step further. No matter what an alcoholic tells you he would rather you do, when he is into putting you down, it really doesn't make any difference to him at all. In other words, you'll *always* be damned if you do and damned if you don't.

This is a most important concept to remember for your peace of mind. What it means, specifically, is that he will only be telling you that he does not like what you are doing (when he is into his 'junk' behavior) in order to get to your jugular.

And when he feels good, he still doesn't care one iota about what he complained about when he was on a binge of putting you down.

Defusing his power.

"Well," you say, "that is somewhat helpful, but how do I stop feeling bad about his complaints when he does say them? They do hurt."

Through family treatment, you will learn another aspect of detachment from his disease that will give you peace of mind around this, too. You will learn to literally wear blinders when he says his junk and eventually, you will, from your heart, *know* he is wrong.

This, in turn, will be picked up by his radar. He will know, instinctively, that his jabbing will not have the effect he wants, and he will lessen it, and eventually drop it.

Another wonderful thing you will begin to see is that when you start this journey of self-trust, you will do things he used to say annoyed him, and when he intuitively knows you are well-grounded in *your* liking of doing it, he will *join* you, and praise you for doing the very things that he used to say were terrible!

Remember, when you are being "got to" by your "ex," and your self-trust is jeopardized, and depression sets in, keep your eyes set on the long haul of detachment from his disease-talk. When he begins to see the *pattern* of your self-trust setting in, he will absolutely back off.

Every spouse tells me "this won't work" with *her* ex-spouse! She tells me, "This one is powerful." She thinks he will see through her getting well; that he will never back off; that he will punish her for getting well; that he can do anything he wants; that he will fool the world forever.

She always thinks that *he* is the powerful one, and forgets that his *disease* is the powerful one talking. The *disease* is trying to intimidate her into getting discouraged, so that it can win. The *disease* knows the power of the healing process. That's why it works so hard, through your "ex's" mouth, to discourage you from trusting your treatment.

What we've been talking about is illusions. Illusions in the alcoholic home. We must, in order to get well from the scars forced on us, begin to see the truth: that everything *is upside-down in the alcoholic home.* Craziness is the norm!

One way to see this clearly is to call the disease's bluff. Pretend you welcomed the alcoholic's playing Santa to the kids! As a result, he will become disoriented, and the totally outlandish gifts will most likely stop, since they were only continuing to come because they "got to you." They started off as guilt-gifts, but they would have stopped naturally if they hadn't become ways to get you to jump when he said jump.

You can't lose. He most probably will lessen the Santa-playing drastically when you pretend you don't care. You will feel an added bonus when you realize you are gaining strength and *not* caring, because you first pretended you didn't care! You are getting out from under, no longer jumping when he cracks the whip.

When the child threatens to leave

What if your child threatens to go live with your ex-spouse or another relative, when you tell him he must go to treatment?

Let's list and sort the fears so they are easier to deal with. You are afraid that . . .

- You ex-spouse will gloat.
- You will feel like a failure.
- Your child will more quickly develop his addiction, living with a constantly drinking parent.

132

- You will be proven wrong. Your child and ex-spouse were right when they said that "they'd be okay if it wasn't for you." They will flourish, apart from you, and you will fall apart.
- If your child goes to live with another relative who will rescue him from the consequences of his disease, and cover up for him, you will look like a fool, and a failure as a parent.
- That *no* one will ever see your child's alcoholism; that *no* one will ever see your ex-spouse's alcoholism; that everyone will always see your "ex" as charming, and you as disturbed.

Let's deal with the "I'll feel like a failure" issue, first. Your child's going or not going to live with someone else who will (temporarily) be conned is no more nor less serious than any other symptom of alcoholism that he displays.

Alcoholism will show itself in any form: cunning, sweet-talking, threats, tears, running. This is but another form of running—running to stay addicted. It has nothing to do with you. You could be a saint of a parent, and if your child, for now, is going to stay addicted, he needs to protect his supply. He believes that the person to whom he is running will help him continue drinking or drugging.

Will your child's addiction proceed faster, if he goes to live with his drinking father? Again, the answer is that your child's addiction has needs of its own.

Alcoholism is a progressive disease. That is, he will need more alcohol at certain points in his disease. At other times, he will seem to need less. So, if he stays, or goes, or goes back and forth, he will consume as much alcohol as he needs at the point where his addiction is, regardless of who he is living with.

What about the other people your child may run to? Will they eventually *see* your child's alcoholism?

The answer is, whether it's with this rescuer or the next, the disease *will* show itself to everyone. And it usually doesn't take that long. I have seen these stages happen over and over again:

1. The child goes to live with an "understanding" aunt or grandmother who believes he just "needs more love than he's getting!"

2. The relative does a lot of fussy gloating.

3. This is followed by a period of frantic-ness: the crises have set in for them, now, too. (It only takes at the most three weeks usually for the "good behavior" to wear itself thin.)

4. The relative will blame you for "setting this child up to have such misery."

5. The relative will demand your time, money, and help.

6. The relative will finally begin to see through it all, in small glimpses, and ask you how you stood it all these years.

7. Each of these steps will repeat, over and over, for years and years— unless you stop your end of it, with a lot of help from Al-Anon and counseling.

The less you attach to the guilt, the less you pay attention to this never-ending drama, the less you allow these relatives to call you in the middle of the night (it's okay to hang up on tirades!)—the more you throw the ball back in the lap of *that* household. And then, the more *they* will be able to see the truth!

The less verbal contact about the sickness that they have with you, the more they will be able to see the disease. The more you allow them to talk with you about it, the more they will dump on you, and not pay attention to the disease. Sure, they'll get angry when you refuse to discuss it, but if you pay no attention to that anger, they will have to turn their attention to the alcoholism and *see* it.

And, when they *see* it, they will be closer to letting go of your child's disease. Then, *he'll* have a chance to own it, and get help for it.

What happens when you start legal proceedings against your spouse, and fear of losing him forever makes you want to drop the case?

First of all, almost everyone goes through this. So, there is no need to feel shame for these feelings of vacillation. I *know* you've told everyone that "he's impossible and you want out." But what will they say? It does not matter! People who don't live with alcoholism don't understand. In the future, it might be more beneficial to only discuss alcoholism craziness with Al-Anon members, those in your recovery group, or your therapist.

Also, keep this in mind: You don't have to be absolutely sure of something in order to act. One can, and often does, have doubts.

But what if your lawyer "screams" at you? Who is paying whom? It is just fine to be the consumer you are, and hire an attorney who is *nice*. We no longer live in the 50's when doctors and lawyers were like gods, never to be asked questions or contradicted.

When you begin to allow yourself the *right* to go back and forth on such a heavy issue as divorce, you will find yourself much more certain of each step. But that only happens when you begin to allow yourself to be what and how you are, today, with all your mixed feelings.

When legal action becomes necessary.

One of the hardest problems to deal with is when your "ex" gets custody or visitation rights, even if he or she is violent, still drinking, and drives drunk with your child in the car.

What I suggest is that you go to the nearest AA meetings, and ask around for attorneys or judges who are in AA who understand alcoholism, and who can advise you on what to do. Each state has different and changing laws; and more and more judges are becoming aware of alcoholism and its many faces.

Plus, don't forget that *you* can report any drunk driver to the police. Especially if your child is in the car.

Reflection/Action Guide

Write On:

1. Look back on the past three days. Write about an important instance when you thought your feelings were not as important as other people's.

2. Write out all your feelings concerning being constantly barraged by your ex-spouse playing Santa with the kids.

3. Write out your feelings about having to be a parent alone; and your "ex" telling you that you are too competent.

4. Write out all the good, *logical* answers to all these situations you've described, in the light of what you've just read in this chapter.

5. Write out your thinking process when you believe that your alcoholic ex-spouse is the powerful one, rather than the disease.

6. Write the response to those feelings.

Suggested Activity:

Keep a record of verbal contacts with the rescuers if your drinking child goes to live with a relative. See if it doesn't correspond to what you've just read in this chapter.

TWELVE

SURROUNDED BY ALCOHOLISM: IF YOUR SPOUSE AND CHILDREN ARE ALL ALCOHOLIC

Samantha, forty-four, is married to a "raging, late-stage" alcoholic, and is the mother of three alcoholics: the oldest two, a boy and a girl, are away at college and her youngest boy is fifteen. Her youngest daughter insists that she "has no problems." This "no-problem" child, Georgina, is ten-and-a-half, very bright, very precocious, and sips wine with the guests when they visit.

Samantha is a professor of economics at a well-known university. Her husband, Karl, despite the progression of his alcoholism, manages to hold on to his position in one of the world's leading companies. His genius at turning many potentially losing situations into very profitable ones encourages his colleagues to ignore his drinking. They are afraid of alienating him, or even angering him into leaving the company and going over to the competition. Samantha has very mixed feelings about his job. She fears that he'll lose it, and that they'll have to alter their lifestyle drastically. She also fears that he *won't* lose it. Then, he'd "be right," and that "she is crazy" when she calls him an alcoholic.

She breathed a big sigh of relief when her oldest children went off to college. She had been through five years of hell at home with them all. There was no way she could do anything to confront their drinking, or use the threat of withholding college tuition in order to get any one of them to go to treatment.

My heart went out to her. I could understand her exhaustion. It is so easy to stand on the sidelines and say to a parent, "Now, if you really cared, you would do this or that." Baloney! This woman did her very best. Probably even more than her best. Just her *surviving* in that household was incredible! There were daily crises. Most days, there were three to seven crises of varying intensity. Before she got to a family-support group, every small problem was terribly mangnified. It was only after one-and-a-half years of attending family recovery sessions, sometimes two or three times a week, that she was able to start seeing the situation more clearly. She began to be able to let go of the smaller problems, to focus on only dealing with the big ones. She began to allow herself to leave the house when the screaming started, going for a drive, a walk or shopping. She also bought headphones and listened to music instead of the insane diatribes.

When you looked at Samantha, you'd never think there was a problem in her life, much less in her entire family. Always fashion conscious and made-up beautifully, she and her family could have posed for a magazine cover. Unfortunately, it would have been appropriate for that magazine to be entitled "Families in Trouble."

Sam (as she called herself) told me she was a little ashamed of how she looked; and at the same time, rather proud of it. "Isn't it denial, to look like nothing is wrong?" she questioned.

I told her I felt that *any* way she survived was wonderful. And that perhaps that was one of her tools for actually surviving so well. At least, *one* thing in her life remained normal.

Sam told me how, now that the older children were away, she felt more capable of dealing with her younger child's addiction. But she said she felt ashamed that she was "abandoning" the older children's needs, that she had 'ignored' thier alcoholism in past years.

I assured Sam that millions of people found that the way they were able to begin dealing with the insanity of a whole household of alcoholics, was to focus on only coping with one alcoholic at a time.

Jim owns his own business in the Southwest. Pamela, his wife of fifteen years, is alcoholic, as is their thirteen-year-old son, Tommie.

Their eleven-year-old daughter, Susanne, is just beginning to display signs of addiction. Jim is disgusted, wants to run, feels surrounded and trapped.

Jim's mother was alcoholic and so was his father. His wife, Pamela, seemd like a lot of fun before they got married and before he saw the ugly side of her drinking.

Now, Tommie, their thirteen-year-old, was drinking and smoking pot and getting to Jim's jugular the same way Pamela could. There were moments when he really hated his child. The shame he felt about his hate, and about wanting to hurt a person half his size, kept him from getting the help he needed. He was so sure that a counselor would put him down for these very *normal* feelings. I could see that one of the worst things for him about his family's drinking was that it still always surprised him.

His "insanity" was the he *believed* his wife and his son when they said "it wouldn't happen again." *Of course* he wanted to believe them! But, it set him up for such disappointment—such rage and anguish.

I suggested that he try to *expect* them to drink, for the time being. This is not "letting them get away with it"—this idea of *expecting* them to drink.

"They'll just figure, 'Good—now, he'll let me alone, and I can drink and drug to my heart's desire!' " Jim argued.

I answered, "Jim, let me show you how this works. This tactic gets two things accomplished. It lets you get relief from their problem, and it will make them very scared about their drinking."

Here's how it works:

- Your wife and child tell you that it'll be different this time.

- You don't say anything. You just tell yourself, "Remember the facts."

You haven't set yourself up for disappointment. They're going to do what they were going to do anyway—whether or not they told you that they wouldn't drink—*and* whether or not you believe it. They drink. It's no different from how it was for the last number of years, no matter what is promised. You're just not going to appear to be a patsy, by believing their baloney.

You aren't feeling betrayed because you weren't down 'in there' with them believing them, and feeling like you were fooled. You *knew* what would happen this time.

You uneasily tell yourself, "Yeah, but, now they'll think I condone their drinking."

But, how you come off is *nonchalant*—not caring whether they drink or not. You do not come off, in their eyes, as a condoner or a condemner of their drinking. You are not mentioning it; you are not listening to or believing or not believing what they say; you are pretending (the real feelings will come later) that you no longer care what they do about their disease. You *act* as if you have finally caught on to the fact that this is not your problem! That you are not the one who is drinking yourself to death! That you aren't a fool, anymore, in your eyes, or in theirs. That *you* don't have to hurt because *they* drink: Let *them* suffer their hangovers alone!

When Jim saw how this process worked, it was so much easier to do what he needed to do.

His wife got furious that he was so detached from her disease the she "threatened" to go to AA to show him he couldn't hold that over her head anymore and act so indifferent about whether she lived or died!

After she was sober awhile, together they intervened and made their son go to treatment. He's now in a halfway house.

Fear of being left.

Most spouses and parents of alcoholics that I've counseled tell me that they had tremendous guilt about the fact that because they were so fearful of the possibility that their alcoholic spouse would leave them (for whatever reason), that they either did not notice the depth of their children's problem, or it took second place in priority. I very strongly believe that this ambivalent reaction to family alcoholism is *totally* normal.

No one escapes the terrors of family alcoholism when you are living in the diseased family! And those terrors are your manifestation of the disease! Don't put yourself in a double bind. Don't blame yourself for having the symptoms of this family disease as well as having to get well from it.

How do you get out from under the immobilizing feelings that come from living with both a spouse and children who are alcoholics?

If you allow yourself to be afraid without putting yourself down for being afraid, your fear will start to dissipate. Stop fighting *yourself* for having the symptoms, and save your energy for fighting the *disease*—and you will begin to see you are not so powerless.

AA says that alcoholism is "cunning, baffling, and powerful."

Yes, it is. It is so cunning that it comes out of the mouths of alcoholics, and makes us think that *they* are powerful—that *they* are to be feared—and we back off.

It is so baffling that it makes otherwise normal-thinking spouses of alcoholics, mothers of alcoholics, fathers of alcoholics, believe that *you* are the crazy ones, the ones with the faulty judgments. It is so cunning and baffling that it makes families half-believe the alcoholic when he or she claims that alcohol is not the problem.

Try doing what a friend of mine did when she visited her husband in the detox center. He is a psychologist, and an alcoholic. Whenever they argued about alcohol, he used his skills as a therapist (even when he was drunk) and he was able to convince her that *he* was the reasonable one, and that *she* was the patient.

After a few sessions of family treatment, however, she told me, "I was able to go visit him when he was in the treatment center, and when he still spoke to me in that social-worker tone of voice, I would start to feel helpless and enraged. And then, I remembered: *He* was the one wearing the pajamas!"

Reflection/Action Guide

Write On:

1. Do you see "early-stage" alcoholism as it is; that it is *alcoholism* as much as is late-stage alcoholism? Do you see that alcoholism exists on a continuum, and not in separated stages?

2. What are some of the ways you have been able to do well in your life despite the alcoholism all around you?

3. Write about some of your feelings that you thought were "wrong," and that now you realize are very normal?

4. Figure out, on paper, how many years your alcoholic child (and spouse) have been telling you "It'll be different this time."

Suggested Activity:

Spend thirty minutes this week viewing the alcoholics in your household as "persons you are observing for signs and symptoms of alcoholism." See if this gives you some distance from the junk that comes out of their mouths.

THIRTEEN

RECOVERING ALCOHOLICS DEAL WITH THEIR CHILDREN'S ALCOHOLISM

Thomas is fifty-two-years old, nineteen years sober, and believes that his next-to-youngest son "isn't an alcoholic" because "he's a good kid."

Some people, after reading this, might point a finger, and say, "Aha! Denial!"—as if denial were a conscious, deliberate avoiding of the truth.

I believe that these parents are acting quite naturally, and lovingly. They *want* the best for their children. They *know* how difficult it is to be an alcoholic. They *wish* it were not so. Even when admitting to the alcoholism, their mixed feelings come out not as mixed *feelings*, but as not believing the whole truth.

Denial doesn't mean striding about, chin up, refusing to see what you obviously do see. It is a terror; brief glimpses of reality; and a retreat into the fog of unknowing so that the pain may stop.

But, what does this unknowing *do* to us? What does it do to the alcoholics we love? Let's look at Maysee.

Maysee (not her real name) is fifty-seven years old, and fifteen years sober, in Alcoholics Anonymous. She also works as a therapist in private practice, helping other recovering alcoholics. She told me that her "three daughters are alcoholic but they're not in active alcoholism

147

yet" and "my kids say 'they can control it.' "

She knows her daughters are drinking. She knows they've gotten into trouble over it (hence her saying she knows they are alcoholic). She knows that both she and her husband of thirty years are alcoholics, therefore, the kids have close to 100 percent chance of becoming alcoholics if they drink.

She says that they're not in active alcoholism yet, but in the next sentence, she says they are controlling their drinking, which means they *are* drinking. Which means they *are* active in their alcoholism, albeit not necessarily a late stage of it. And she also knows that social drinkers do not go around claiming to be able to control their drinking. It's just not that important to them—they don't think about it that much—they don't think about it at all! They don't bother controlling it.

But what does this line of thinking do to Maysee? When she is with her children, she often is churning inside. She is torn between what she wishes, and what she sees. She feels that much of the time she must hold in her thoughts and feelings. She does not want to alienate her children by preaching at them. She, and they, want to pretend it does not happen, and that "it" will "just go away by itself."

I am not advocating a constant talking about alcoholism, but it is a matter of reinforcing inside *us*, first, our belief that it is a disease, and not a shame. When I see loved ones killing themselves with alcohol or drugs, I must constantly tell myself, when I get tight in my stomach, that part of this tightness is my feelings about the stigma of alcoholism. And *that* comes from the part of me that has not totally accepted that this is a disease.

And part of that non-acceptance of the disease concept is my feeling that this person's anger makes *him* very powerful. It is my forgetting that the *disease* is the powerful, cunning, and baffling thing—not the suffering alcoholic. That the anger and threats coming from their mouths is the *disease* telling me to back off, to have mixed feelings, to be afraid of it and afraid of the alcoholic.

When we begin to accept, in *ourselves*, all those terribly important ramifications of the disease concept—then we send the alcoholic certain messages.

- That we feel certain, in our eyes, and in God's, that we are allowed, without guilt, to end the rescue operations that we were formerly trapped in.

- That we know that this will *help* the alcoholic as nothing else can.

- That we know that we do not, any longer, have to stand around and listen to the child's *disease* talking—that we have permission, now, to leave the room or house, or just tune out.

- That we are freed from the guilt that "we somehow set the stage" for his or her alcoholism.

These long-term, lasting benefits, for the alcoholic's sobriety, and for the parent's peace of mind, come from an inner knowledge that it is okay and important to no longer deny the alcoholism.

One winter afternoon in downtown Chicago, I talked at brunch with several recovering alcoholics in AA. Sandra told me that "no matter how much I tell myself it is a disease, part of me doesn't believe it. I guess I don't want to believe it—don't ask me why. I don't know. I guess there's some deep-seated sick reason for why I don't want 'off the hook,' but I guess that's just it. I feel like it's letting us off the hook, and we don't deserve to be. It's like we were bad people, and deserve to be forever punished."

I believe alcoholics have a choicce. A choice to continue thinking, despite all the medical evidence, that alcoholism is a moral problem, the choice to continue to feel lousy during recovery, or the choice to make that tough decision to learn how to live differently, and be happy. For many alcoholics, this is one of the toughest decisions ever.

I believe that that's part of what AA means when it says that in order to totally recover, alcoholics must make a 180-degree turn in thinking. To make a conscious decision to believe, and act like one believes, that God is a loving God, and that the time for punishment is over. But I don't think we get to that point until we are sick and tired of being sick and tired.

Getting rid of false guilt.

Michael told me how much guilt he felt when he remembered that he used to send his little girl, when she was seven, to fetch beer from the fridge for him. She's now fifteen, and drinking a lot.

Sam told how he used to take his son around with him when he was eleven or twelve years old, to different bars. He'd introduce him to all his buddies, telling them how smart his son was, how good he was in all his school subjects. He'd glow with all that attention. Sam said, "I set him up to like the bars."

I asked Michael and Sam if they believed that their children would have become alcoholics even if they, the parents, had been perfect examples.

"Yeah, I guess so," they both answered.

"Let me ask it this way," I said. "Do you think they could have become alcoholics *as easily* if you had been perfect?"

"No," they both answered immediately.

"Why?"

Sam answered, "I think I showed him a very Bohemian existence that he's tried to live ever since."

Marcia interjected with her experience. "I've often wondered where my husband's alcoholism came from. He was raised by teetotaling Baptists. They didn't even have a deck of cards in the house, much less a bottle of beer. Three of their five sons are alcoholics."

Then, Sam said, "You know, you're right. I couldn't have had a blander father. He was the complete opposite of me! *I* certainly didn't turn out bland! I chased excitement! So he didn't make me into an alcoholic! Maybe I didn't 'make' my son into an alcoholic!"

Marcia continued, "Besides, we're less important as a total role-model than we think. When *we* grew up, there certainly weren't the drugs, and no one drank so openly, so early, as these kids do. So, there *is* peer pressure. It's not just *our* example."

"It occurs to me," I reflected, "listening to you all, that you're always asking a lot of yourselves. You're not only dealing with your own alcoholism, but you also feel you must always have this wonderful, dispassionate, saint-like attitude toward your child."

"Yeah!" Marcia agreed. "That 'walking on eggs' will cure him! It's that guilt again, creeping back in. 'If only I hadn't been an alcoholic myself, he'd be all right.' So, I'd better 'make up' for it all, and be wonderful, at all times, and not allow myself to be human, and get angry. After all, 'if I'm an alcoholic, I better understand how he feels, and always be loving and kind even when I want to scream at him!'"

We met four more times. The sharing, finally telling each other of the guilt and the anger, brought a tremendous relief. I never met with them again, but I hear that they keep in touch with each other. Some go to Al-Anon; some don't. But they don't hold those feelings in any longer. And it's not at all as frightening as it used to be.

Action/Reflection Guide

Write On:

1. Do you find yourself wanting to maintain a "hard-edged" image for yourself—telling yourself that this problem "doesn't bother you" as much as it really does?

2. Do you talk to others about it, and not keep it bottled up?

3. Does it seem "wrong" to go to Al-Anon for help; that AA "should be enough"?

4. If you have gone to Al-Anon, despite the welcome you received there, were you uncomfortable because you are an alcoholic?

5. Do you feel you are betraying your fellow AA's when you go to Al-Anon and participate in "talking about alcoholics"?

6. Do you see ways of resolving this? Do you see how what you learn in family treatment can help your child *and* you?

Suggested Activity:

Begin talking about these issues you just wrote about, with other parents who have gone to family treatment. Ask them specifically how Al-Anon or counseling helped them.

FOURTEEN

NO NEED FOR SHAME
IF YOUR CHILD
IS VIOLENT

"I want to run! But, they'll kill each other. I'd better stay, and protect them. But I'm half their size."

The above words came from a woman who is both the spouse and the mother of violent, drinking alcoholics.

Why hasn't she told even me, her counselor, about this violence before now?

"I'm so ashamed," she said. "Since kids respect their parents, if he does hit me, they'll all think there *is* a reason for him to hit me."

This woman lives in fear, isolated.

Living alone with an abusive alcoholic child.

Another type of mother believes she is just all anger and no guilt, and says, "*Go* to live with your father! See if *he'll* put up with it! Him and that new wife of his, *they* won't put up with it for a minute!"

She talks fast, compulsively, to any stranger who will listen: the typist at the next desk, the women at the bus stop in the morning, the bank teller.

She has no idea that her unconscious guilt won't let her really believe that she has the right not to be abused. She'd scoff at the assumption that she has any guilt. Calls herself a strong Irish mother and has worked all her life. Her children *were* her life.

She is shocked, not wanting to believe the violent drinking bouts of her "pride and joy"—her son.

She thought she could recapture the early years when they adored each other. It was her and him against his father, when his father drank and verbally abused everyone. Her son stood up to him. Now, her son has joined him.

Acknowledging the fears.

Nobody, absolutely nobody, can make a move to get out from under a terrible situation, or be able to help someone they love to get help, until they acknowledge to themselves that there are understandable terrors to overcome.

But once you acknowledge these terrors, you've gone more than 75 percent of the way toward getting rid of them completely. It's our pride—and *all* of us are ruled by our pride at times in our lives—that stops us from acknowledging those terrible fears.

What are some of these feelings and fears?

- Feelings of betrayal.

- Feelings of terrible shame.

- Guilt about our anger towards the child who is hitting us.

- Guilt about *thoughts* of wanting to be "irresponsible" and run away from home.

- Hurt about the collusion between the alcoholic child and the alcoholic parent.

- Terrors about the isolation you feel in not believing you can talk about this with anyone.

- Despair that you'll never get out of this black hole.

- Fear of what others will think.

Getting away from the above.

The last thing in the world you need is for someone to say to you, "Why do you put up with it?"

I am always amazed when counselors often blithely mouth that they know of the terrible fears that prevent clients from leaving abuse—and then turn around and ask the client, "Why do you stay?"

I can only surmise that people who have not experienced the depth of the terrors experienced by victims of abuse cannot relate to how much those experiences have totally emotionally beaten that person down. An abused client *cannot* take steps to change at the same rate as a person who has not gone through abuse.

People who live with alcoholism, especially people whose spouses and children are alcoholics, or whose parents were alcoholics and whose children are now, can't start at Point A and proceed to Point Z in just six months of counseling.

Their self-esteem is so low that it will take them many months in counseling before they are even ready to begin making progress.

But, there's hope. Once their progress has started, and if they are working with a counselor who understands the need to totally accept the client's vacillation (returning to the abusive situation, *repeatedly*) as part and parcel of the progress, then the client has about a one hundred percent chance of getting well!

Finding hope for the future

What more can you do both to help calm down the situation, and have real hope for the future?

Go to Al-Anon. Go to counseling.

We're dealing with a disease that is more powerful than any one of us, alone. I'm sure you can recall many incidents where a crisis happened; you reacted with fear and anger; you threatened the alcoholic (be it leaving or throwing them out); maybe you left or made them leave; you came back, or begged them to return; you felt despairing, depressed, and humiliated.

This cycle is what most of us go through in alcoholic homes. You are not alone.

Add to this the shame we feel for "acting like maniacs" in our homes, when many of us are, to the outside world, competent professionals and responsible homemakers. We often feel like two people.

Don't avoid getting help.

We tend to avoid helping groups when we need help the most, for four basic reasons. Let's consider each briefly:

1. **We think no one knows, and that if we go for treatment, "everyone will know."**

   When I was a little girl my father was a drinking alcoholic. After he'd stumble through the doors, my mother would say, "He's drunk again," and lock the doors and pull down the shades. Obviously, she thought those acts shielded our household from shame, and that way, the neighbors wouldn't know. Who in the world did she think was fooled? He'd already stumbled in the door!

   I had a rude awakening, in the same vein. Years ago, when I got over growing up in a small town with my father "making us ashamed," I decided to get in touch with an old high school friend whom I had not seen in years.

   I called her and after a few minutes of surprised greetings, I asked, "Sally, did you know my father was an alcoholic?" She answered matter-of-factly: "Of course." After realizing how amazed I was that she knew so readily, I was even more shocked that, like my mother, I had assumed they really didn't know.

   We are full of contradictions. We are ashamed and believe we successfully kept others from knowing. Yet, we walk around, looking at the ground, assuming that everyone does know.

2. **We want to believe it will all "go away" by itself. This is bolstered by remorse of the alcoholic whom we want to believe when he says "I'll never do it again."**

   He *does* mean it. He *is* ashamed. But the *disease* won't allow him to stop, as long as he is drinking—even "a little."

3. **We fear that we brought it on ourself. All battered women feel that way. This belief (along with the "It'll be different this time" belief) keeps more women in battering situations than anything else. That, and the fear of losing the alcoholic.**

   He threatens. He says if you go to treatment, he'll leave because "you are telling the community that he's an alcoholic." Or, if it weren't for your behavior (your "nagging," "screaming," "bitching," "cleaning all the time," "not cleaning enough," "religious fanaticism," and so on) he wouldn't get so mad that you force him to hit you.

Tell a person, enough times, over enough months and years, that they are the cause of their own persecution, and they either start to believe it or fight believing it. If they fight believing it, they eventually need to question why they are staying with this person who is trying to destroy their soul.

The next step, in order to maintain some order in their minds and to allay the anxiety about why they are choosing to stay with an abuser is that they will partially tell themselves that he *is* saying the truth, that they *are* the cause of their own persecution, therefore laying the mind-conflict to rest. Of course, at the expense of their self-respect, at the least.

4. **With a child (even though that "child" might be a foot taller than you), the conflict is much stronger than it is with a spouse.**

All kinds of blood-ties and parental guilt gets in the way. It can be gently untangled, in counseling or in Al-Anon, but it takes time. We have to allow ourselves time to heal, time to begin to view ourselves as children of God who have innate rights not to be hit, shoved, or negatively treated.

What I believe is going on, in that thought process of fear of abandonment, is that we are the products of a sick alcoholism that tells us, insidiously, that we are very, very "little," and that the alcoholic is very, very "big." That even though the alcoholic may be sixteen-years-old, he holds much of our self-esteem in his hand. In the healing process, we slowly begin to realize that we are as big as other people; that we are normal-sized, and that our survival skills are as big as other people's. We have begun to lose our fear of people.

This process, once it has begun, has incredibly wonderful ramifications:

- We lose our fear that the alcoholic is holding us together, emotionally.

- We "get bigger."

- The alcoholic "gets normal-sized."

159

- We begin to see the "junk behavior" in perspective.

- We take interest in ourselves and the outside world again.

- This healthy detachment from the disease begets more healthy detachment.

- We go to sleep, watch TV, read and just relax when the alcoholic storms out.

- We are amazed, relieved, and delighted that we have been given back our lives.

- One day, the alcoholic sees that we truly do not care about his disease: that it is not our problem any more.

- The alcoholic gets scared about our detachment, owns his own disease, and has a chance to choose sobriety.

Now, don't think this is all happening in one happy, straight line! It will most probably involve much yelling, screaming, fretting, and thinking that you're not making any progress in treatment. Surprising periods of peace will be followed by manic-times; followed by more peace. And so the cycle will repeat until the healing is complete. Be patient and gentle with yourself, yet be quietly persistent and determined to find the healing *you* need.

Once you choose to get help, you have *no* way to go but to feel better, to heal and to feel intact, emotionally, perhaps for the first time ever. And the alcoholic will finally have a good chance to choose sobriety.

Reflection/Action Guide

Write On:

1. Divide a paper in half, lengthwise. On one side, list what is going on in your home. On the other, how the "community" sees your family members. Let yourself remember the facts, as you have written them, when you start to berate yourself for "craziness," when you hear outsiders tell you that nothing is wrong in your home.

2. Write down what your alcoholic family members tell you when you have been abused; i.e., "you made me do it." Write down the truth—now.

3. If a very good friend had the same happen to her, write what you would tell her to think, feel, and do.

4. Write out how your survival skills are just as competent and effective as other people's.

Suggested Activities:

1. Each time you tell yourself, "What did I do to bring it on?" and "It'll be different next time," tell yourself that the disease is talking.

2. Each time you think you cannot, for any reason at all, live without that alcoholic in your life, remind yourself how your survival skills are just as competent and effective as other people's.

3. Go to Al-Anon; consider joining a battered women's group.

HOT LINE NUMBERS AND OTHER RESOURCES

Each of the following organizations listed below represent many adolescent treatment programs, all over the country. A call to any of them will put you in touch with the center nearest you.

- Addiction Recovery Centers—1-800-822-0223
- Charter Medical Corp.—1-800-845-1567
- CompCare Corp.—1-800-854-0318
- HCA (Hospital Corp. of America)—1-800-251-2561
- Mediplex Corp.—1-800-451-1716 (N.Y. & New England)
- New Day Centers—1-800-447-5471
- Brookwood—205-877-1835
- Healthcare International—714-838-9600, ext. 4000
- Koala Centers—717-538-2567
- Parkside Medical Services Corp.—312-698-4700
- Psychiatric Hospitals of America—215-836-1380
- Recovery Centers of America—202-298-3230

> In addition to the above numbers, there are many fine local facilities all over the country, that specialize in kids and alcoholism. See the ads in your telephone directories under "alcoholism" and when calling, make sure they treat alcoholism as a *primary disease*, and not as the result of mental health issues.

OTHER NUMBERS TO HAVE

- National Federation of Parents for Drug-Free Youth
  1-800-554-KIDS
- Families in Crisis (they will come to your home and do an intervention for you)—612-893-1883
- For the numbers of AA, Al-Anon, NA (Narcotics Anonymous), Al-Ateen, and Nar-Anon (for parents of drug addicts), ask your telephone operator. Call these groups for meeting schedules and free literature.

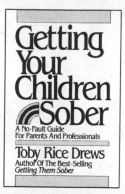

Getting Your Children Sober
A No-Fault Guide For Parents And Professionals
Toby Rice Drews
Author Of The Best-Selling *Getting Them Sober*

THIRTY MINUTE VIDEO

Featuring
Toby Rice Drews

Purchase price: $395

A short "disposable" preview
videotape featuring highlights
is available for $20.
This fee is deductible from
the purchase price.

To order, write:

Maryland Publishing Company
P.O. Box 19910
Baltimore, MD 21211

Or call: (301) 243-8558